Poolside Cooking™

More than just a cookbook; it's a lifestyle!

Jemmalyn Hewlett

with

Alesha R. Brown

Poolside Cooking™: More than just a cookbook; it's a lifestyle!

©2025 Jemmalyn Hewlett

This work was compiled and written in collaboration with Alesha R. Brown of Fruition Publishing Concierge Services®, serving as ghostwriter, publishing strategist, and creative director.

Published in Hampton, VA, by Fruition Publishing Concierge Services®. Fruition Publishing Concierge Services® is a division of Alesha Brown, LLC.

Fruition Publishing Concierge Services® can bring authors to your live event. For more information or to book an event, visit Fruition Publishing Concierge Services® at:

www.FruitionPublishing.com

ISBN: 978-1-954486-58-4 eBook

ISBN: 978-1-954486-64-5 Paperback

ISBN: 978-1-954486-59-1 Hardcover

Library of Congress Control Number: 2024927634

Contents

PREFACE

Poolside Cooking™ goes beyond being a mere cookbook; it embodies a way of life. This book takes readers on a visionary journey led by serial entrepreneur Jemmalyn Hewlett, showcasing how a pool and the art of poolside cuisine can bring together diverse communities. From politicians and artists to nonprofit founders and small business owners, Poolside Cooking™ serves as a catalyst for unity.

But this book is more than just a collection of poolside recipes for all seasons. It is a captivating narrative that delves into the essence of success. By intricately weaving the stories of individuals featured in the Poolside Cooking™ TV Show, readers gain invaluable insights into the recipe for achieving their own success.

In the spirit of community and shared experiences, we invite you to connect with us at PoolsideCookingShow.com. Share your thoughts, subscribe to our channel, and spread the joy by introducing our platform to your friends. Your feedback is incredibly valuable to us, so please take a moment to leave a review on barnesandnoble.com, amazon.com, our social media pages, and any online platform where you purchased our book. We sincerely appreciate your support.

Wishing you great success,

Admin, Poolside Cooking LLC

PoolsideCookingShow.com

FOREWORD
The Recipe of Success

By Jemmalyn Hewlett

I can honestly say that the vision of Poolside Cooking and being a serial entrepreneur were not on my radar. Neither was having the #1 Poolside Cooking TV Show in Virginia. But I am the picture of what a determination bred by desperation and life's struggles can birth.

My serial entrepreneurial story did not start with the Poolside Cooking™ TV Show or any parts of the platform. It actually started with WeCare Medical Transport.

In 2011, I was a mother with two children that was struggling. I was struggling financially and trying to figure out what I wanted to do in life. I was working at a medical school making under $20,000 a year and decided that I needed to make a change.

What made me start a business? For me, the answer is simple: I was tired of being broke. WeCare Medical Transport wasn't something I went to college for. It wasn't something that I aspired to do. I was simply tired of being broke! Can you relate?

So, I made a change; a BIG one. I started We Care Medical Transport. Historically, women are rare in any part of the transportation industry, and I was still trying to understand and learn the business. More than a decade later, I can tell you this: you will make mistakes regardless of your education, knowledge, and background, but YOU can fix all of them. That is the beauty of business. The problem is a lot of people go into business thinking that everything is supposed to be perfect or go according to plan. They either don't start or delay starting until they feel everything is perfect and exactly how they want it. That is not how business works.

To be an entrepreneur or successful business owner, you have to **grow** into it. Business is a continual work of finding out what it takes to get to the next level, not a game of perfection. While you wait, opportunity is passing you by. No one can afford that.

So that's exactly what we did in our business: made A LOT of mistakes. Oh, we climbed that ladder, and it wasn't in my best, pretty pair of heels. I had to stop trying to "look cute" as I climbed the ladder and had to put on a pair of sneakers and get down to business. I'm not going to lie: it was a struggle, but a GOOD struggle. I was starting from the bottom and broker then broke: What did I have to lose?

You know the cliché that *ignorance is bliss*? In a way, I guess for me that helped. I didn't understand why I was struggling in business. I felt at the time I was doing everything right. I had to question and ask God why were things going wrong. Well, for one, because I didn't have experience, degree or knowledge, so of course things were going to go wrong, but I also had to understand that everything that went wrong was supposed to happen. Why? because that's how I was able to learn. If you are reading this and currently struggling, I want you to know this:

I had to understand that when I was going through those struggles and things were going wrong, it was simply postage: the price I had to pay for success. How else was I going to learn? It was simply a process that I was going through and, regardless of your level of education, knowledge, and experience, there is a process that you must go through.

Once I learned the business, I realized that my job was to build generational wealth. Talk about an aha moment. I started a business as a struggling mother of two because I was tired of being broke; I knew nothing about that business, and my next thoughts were I needed to build generational wealth? To some this might seem ridiculous, but there is no other option.

This is where my daughter Ashley comes in. I am so proud of her as she grows with me in business, now businesses of her own, because she never questioned or asked why, especially when things went wrong. She just kind of looked at me like *is that supposed to happen*? Next, she would look at me and say, "What do we got to do?"

Because my daughter understood the process, something I was glad she learned firsthand from me, it was easy for me to put her in place to understand and learn the business. That is one thing I love about her: she sits back, watches, listens and then does exactly what I did (probably a little bit better).

The process wasn't something I could explain to her, and I want that to be a lesson for my readers. Of course, we want more for our kids and we want to make sure that they understand that we want them to do better. I could show her everything in business from how the process goes to putting in the application and starting the business. But I couldn't show her the process when something went wrong.

See, that process isn't something that is written in books nor something that you can Google. At that moment I had to learn I was the teacher and the student. That process is between you and God. With his help and guidance, you will learn your process and whether business is for you or not. Entrepreneurship/business ownership, regardless of how much it is glorified, it's not for everyone. If you discover in your journey that it is not for you, do not be ashamed or dismayed. It is okay and not a testament of your worth or inadequacy.

In business, when things were going wrong with me, I knew what I had to do and what I could not handle. But I didn't know what my daughter could handle. I had to let her understand and figure that on her own. And boy did she do exactly that. The roles reversed: I had to sit back and watch how she handled things in business. I told her that the same attitude she had when she was excited about getting that business license is the same attitude she need to have when things go wrong. Watching my daughter, I knew this was for her. She was built for this and if I had not persevered in my journey that was birthed from struggle, I might not have ever seen her venture into entrepreneurship. That is one of the dangers when we let fear hold us back, especially in times of struggle. It is not just our success that we delay or forfeit, it is those that would have been part of the journey if we had done what we were supposed to do.

I'll get to Poolside Cooking™ in a minute, but when I think of my daughter, I'm so proud of her, of what she accomplished. Ashley started WeCare II where, like its parent company, she provides supportive in-home services to individuals with intellectual developmental disabilities. Oh, by the way, she opened up a juice bar too. And, as of the writing of this book, she is the new co-host of the Poolside Cooking™ TV Show. I have shared all of this so you understand that nothing is perfect, but you are fully capable of creating a perfect ending as long as you start. Go through the process, believe in yourself, execute that plan and most importantly, know who's in charge, GOD!

As I taught my daughter, when something happens, don't put your energy on why it happened. Instead, place your energy into figuring out how to fix it. As God's children, we have to use our energy on making things happen, not why things didn't happen. And when things do not go according to plan, which they won't, stand in position knowing you are equipped to fix it.

Last, but not least, I must thank all my staff, current and past, that took this journey with me. WeCare, WeCare Juice Bar, Poolside Cooking™, and Poolside Cooking™ TV show would not be possible without all those who have supported us through the years and continue to do so. However, our staff is why we are still in business. They are the face of our companies, so I cannot emphasize enough that without them, there would be no us. We cannot run this business, this empire by ourselves. As a business owner, you must always be willing to roll up your sleeves and I do. However, I cannot single handedly run a café, be a chef, a waitress, a producer, a juice bar barista, and all the other things on a very long list for a successful business empire. No one can be all those things, yet, I see so many entrepreneurs trying to do exactly that, solo.

It is very important that we put people in place, people that understand and see the vision. The vision might not always be clear to them, but as long as we understand what it is, we all can keep it moving.

I will end on this note: things might not always be easy, but just know that it will be worth it. You cannot give up. You have a legacy and generational wealth to build.

May God's eternal blessings always be upon you,

Jemmalyn Hewlett, Founder/CEO

The Dream Team

Pictured from L to R: Chef Wimbo, Ashley Marie, Jemmalyn Hewlett, Clarence Neely, Curt the Hero, and DJ Jr Rock

Not pictured: Joey Blanco, Videographer/Photographer

Introduction

What is so special about Poolside Cooking™ TV Show?

The Poolside Cooking™ TV Show and platform is distinctive and special for several reasons:

1. Community Building: Poolside Cooking™ goes beyond just recipes; it fosters a sense of community. The emphasis on communal gatherings around a pool creates an environment where people from diverse backgrounds, including politicians, artists, nonprofit founders, and small business owners, come together.

2. Lifestyle Integration: It is not merely about cooking; it's a lifestyle. Poolside Cooking™ integrates the joy of cooking with the relaxing and social atmosphere of a pool, making it a unique and holistic experience.

3. Entrepreneurial Vision: The vision behind Poolside Cooking™, driven by serial entrepreneur Jemmalyn Hewlett, showcases the entrepreneurial spirit. The fusion of business acumen with culinary creativity is a distinguishing factor.

4. Seasonal Adaptability: The recipes cater to every season, making Poolside Cooking™ a versatile culinary guide. Whether it's summer, fall, winter, or spring, there are poolside recipes tailored to each season's atmosphere and ingredients.

5. Personal Stories: What sets Poolside Cooking™ apart is its storytelling aspect. Through the featured personalities and their stories, viewers gain insights into the diverse journeys, challenges, and successes related to both the culinary world and broader life experiences.

6. Online Community Engagement: The platform's active engagement with its audience through the website, social media, and other online channels creates a dynamic community of like-minded individuals who share a passion for poolside cooking.

Poolside Cooking™ and the Poolside Cooking™ TV Show platform is special because it transcends the conventional boundaries of a cookbook, offering a lifestyle that celebrates connection, creativity, and the joy of shared experiences around the pool. Are you ready to go poolside?

The Importance of Community in Poolside Cooking™

The Importance of Community in Poolside Cooking™

Nestled by the glistening waters of the pool, where the sun's embrace meets the gentle ripples, Poolside Cooking™ isn't just a culinary endeavor—it's a communal symphony. This is where the aroma of grilled delicacies intermingles with laughter, where every sizzle and chop harmonizes with stories shared and friendships forged. Here, we celebrate not just the flavors that tantalize our palates, but the essence of community that seasons every dish with love and fellowship.

Jemmalyn Hewlett, the visionary behind the #1 Poolside Cooking™ TV Show in the United States, didn't set out to create a mere cooking show. Her journey, a patchwork of entrepreneurial triumphs and life's trials, was the crucible in which the ethos of Poolside Cooking was forged. It's not about the solitary act of preparing food—it's about the unity and joy that comes from sharing it. It's about politicians discussing policy over prosciutto, artists finding inspiration in antipasti, and nonprofit founders brainstorming better futures between bites of bruschetta.

At its core, Poolside Cooking™ celebrates the intersection of diverse lives and stories. Every episode is a testament to the power of food in bringing people together. The poolside setting, a universal symbol of leisure and luxury, is transformed into a stage for inclusivity. It's where a small business owner's anecdote can resonate with a senator's vision, where the zest of an entrepreneur's tale can add spice to an artist's next masterpiece.

Community is the secret ingredient in every recipe featured on the show. It's the shared platters that invite hands to reach in unison, the communal bowls that serve as vessels for both nourishment and conversation. These recipes aren't mere instructions on a page; they are narratives of the collective experience, memories made tangible through taste and texture.

Jemmalyn's own story mirrors this philosophy. Starting with the seeds of desperation, she cultivated WeCare Medical Transport from the ground up, learning that growth is an ongoing process, not a single harvest. And as she expanded her empire to include the Poolside Cooking™ brand, she brought with her the lessons of resilience, the spirit of innovation, and the conviction that community is integral to success.

But perhaps what truly captures the essence of community in poolside cuisine is the act of cooking itself. It is an act of service, of giving, of creating something with the intention of sharing. It's a language that transcends words, where flavors communicate acceptance and a shared meal becomes a shared journey.

So as we turn the pages of this culinary chronicle, let us remember that Poolside Cooking™ is more than just a method of preparing food. It's a lifestyle, a philosophy, and a testament to the connective power of cuisine. It's an invitation to gather by the pool, to dip our toes into the stories that simmer beneath the surface, and to partake in the feast of fellowship that awaits.

In the world of Poolside Cooking, every meal is a gathering, every dish a dialogue, and every bite a bridge to a stronger, more vibrant community.

Flavor & Recipe Tips

While we've kept each recipe clean and easy to follow, the *Poolside Cooking™* lifestyle is all about elevating every detail—from your ingredients to your atmosphere.

Here are a few ways to make every dish and gathering unforgettable:

1. **Pick the Freshest Produce:** Choose fruits and vegetables that are in season for optimal flavor. Look for vibrant colors, firm textures, and fresh scents—especially when using watermelon, mangoes, citrus, and herbs.

2. **Choose the Right Meats:** For grilling, opt for fresh cuts like wild-caught shrimp, chicken thighs for juiciness, and well-marbled beef for flavor. Trim excess fat and marinate for tenderness and taste.

3. **Drink Pairing Basics:** Light seafood or fruit-based dishes pair well with citrusy white wines, rosés, or spritzers. Rich meats or grilled items balance beautifully with bold red wines, spiced cocktails, or robust beers.

4. **Smart Alcohol Selections:** When choosing alcohol for cocktails, avoid artificially flavored liquors. Go for fresh infusions or quality base spirits. For example, use 100% agave tequila, clean white rum, and botanical gins for smoother, better-tasting drinks.

5. **Presentation Matters:** A beautiful spread enhances appetite. Use colorful platters, tropical leaves, wooden boards, and edible flowers to create a wow factor.

6. **Healthy Swaps:**

- Use Greek yogurt instead of mayo or sour cream.
- Try coconut sugar or honey in place of white sugar.
- Substitute cauliflower rice or zucchini noodles in place of carbs.
- Grill instead of frying for a lighter version.

7. **Diet-Friendly Adjustments:** Offer options that accommodate dietary needs—gluten-free pasta, dairy-free cheeses, and mocktail versions of alcoholic drinks using sparkling water or fresh juice blends.

8. **Make It Yours:** Add your own spin. Mix up fruit combos, spice levels, or garnishes to suit your personal taste or the occasion.

9. **Host Like a Star:** Create a vibe—think music playlists, string lights, themed napkins, and chilled towel service for guests. It's all about the experience!

10. **Share the Flavor:** Capture your creation and tag us at **#PoolsideCooking**. We love seeing your personal touches and delicious results!

Your success is always on the menu.

RECIPES BY THE SEASON

The Poolside Cooking™ TV Show took off so fast that we were faced with an interesting challenge: how do we keep the summer sizzle alive all year round? With a dash of our founder's creativity, we conjured up a solution - an indoor studio mirroring our outdoor breezy poolside set. This innovation ensures that regardless of the season, the show will go on. We even introduced Poolside Cooking™ Cribs, where we toured the kitchens of chefs across America, spicing up your menu with a variety of culinary wonders.

Wondering what to whip up for poolside pleasure regardless of the time of year? We've got you covered with our all-seasons guide.

SUMMER

Food: Embrace the lightness of summer with grilled seafood delights like shrimp and fish, toss up fresh fruit salads, or chill with cold pasta salads. Bite into the juiciness of tropical fruits such as watermelon and pineapple.

Drinks: Quench your thirst with crisp mojitos, refreshing sangria, or the tangy twist of a classic margarita. Light beers and fruity cocktails are the essence of summer revelry.

APPETIZERS & SIDE DISHES
SUMMER

Watermelon and Feta Salad

Ingredients:

- 4 cups of watermelon, cubed
- 1 cup of crumbled feta cheese
- 1/4 cup of fresh mint leaves, chopped
- 2 tablespoons of balsamic glaze
- 1 tablespoon of extra virgin olive oil
- Salt and pepper to taste

1. **Prepare the Watermelon:** Cut the watermelon into bite-sized cubes. Ensure that the watermelon is ripe and juicy for the best flavor.
2. **Combine Ingredients:** In a large bowl, gently toss the watermelon cubes with the crumbled feta cheese and chopped mint leaves.
3. **Season and Dress:** Drizzle the mixture with the extra virgin olive oil. Season with a pinch of salt and pepper to taste. Be cautious with the salt, as feta cheese is already salty.
4. **Serve and Garnish:** Transfer the salad to a serving platter or bowl. Drizzle the balsamic glaze over the top just before serving to add a sweet and tangy contrast.
5. **Optional:** For added texture and flavor, you can sprinkle some toasted pine nuts or almonds on top.

Fresh Tomato and Basil Bruschetta

Ingredients:

- 1 baguette, sliced into 1/2-inch thick slices
- 4-5 ripe tomatoes, diced (about 2 cups)
- 1/4 cup fresh basil leaves, finely chopped
- 3 cloves garlic, minced
- 1/4 cup extra virgin olive oil, plus extra for brushing the bread
- 1 tablespoon balsamic vinegar (optional)
- Salt and pepper to taste
- 1/4 cup grated Parmesan cheese (optional)

1. **Prepare the Tomato Topping:**

- In a medium bowl, combine the diced tomatoes, minced garlic, and chopped basil.
- Drizzle with 1/4 cup of extra virgin olive oil and balsamic vinegar (if using).
- Season with salt and pepper to taste.
- Mix well and let the flavors meld together while you prepare the bread.

2. **Prepare the Baguette Slices:**

- Preheat a grill or grill pan over medium-high heat.
- Brush both sides of the baguette slices lightly with extra virgin olive oil.

3. **Grill the Baguette Slices:**

- Place the oiled baguette slices on the grill.
- Grill for about 2-3 minutes per side, or until they are golden brown and have grill marks. Be careful not to burn them.

4. **Assemble the Bruschetta:**

- Remove the grilled baguette slices from the grill and place them on a serving platter.
- Spoon the tomato mixture generously onto each slice of grilled baguette.
- If desired, sprinkle a small amount of grated Parmesan cheese over the top of each bruschetta for added flavor.

5. **Serve Immediately:**

- Serve the bruschetta immediately while the bread is still warm and crispy.
- Optionally, garnish with additional fresh basil leaves for presentation.

Avocado Mango Salsa

Ingredients:

- 2 ripe avocados, diced
- 2 ripe mangoes, diced
- 1/2 red onion, finely diced
- 1/4 cup fresh cilantro, chopped
- 2 limes, juiced
- 1 jalapeño, finely chopped (optional, for heat)
- Salt and pepper to taste
- Tortilla chips, for serving

1. **Prepare the Ingredients:**

- Dice the avocados and mangoes into bite-sized pieces.
- Finely dice the red onion.
- Chop the fresh cilantro.
- If using, finely chop the jalapeño. Remove seeds for less heat.

2. **Combine the Ingredients:**

- In a medium mixing bowl, gently combine the diced avocados, diced mangoes, red onion, cilantro, and jalapeño (if using).

- Pour the fresh lime juice over the mixture.
- Gently toss to combine, being careful not to mash the avocados too much.

3. **Season and Adjust:**

- Season with salt and pepper to taste.
- Adjust the lime juice, salt, and pepper as needed to achieve your desired flavor balance.

4. **Serve:**

- Transfer the salsa to a serving bowl.
- Serve immediately with tortilla chips.

Minty Melon Salad

Ingredients:

- 2 cups watermelon, balled or cubed
- 2 cups cantaloupe, balled or cubed
- 2 cups honeydew melon, balled or cubed
- 1/4 cup fresh mint leaves, finely chopped
- 2 tablespoons honey or agave syrup
- 1 lime, juiced
- Optional: a pinch of salt

1. **Prepare the Melons:**

- Using a melon baller or a sharp knife, scoop or cut the watermelon, cantaloupe, and honeydew into bite-sized balls or cubes.
- Place all the melon balls or cubes into a large mixing bowl.

2. **Prepare the Dressing:**

- In a small bowl, whisk together the lime juice and honey (or agave syrup) until well combined.

3. **Combine the Ingredients:**

- Pour the lime and honey dressing over the melons in the large mixing bowl.
- Add the finely chopped fresh mint leaves to the bowl.

4. **Toss the Salad:**

- Gently toss all the ingredients together until the melon pieces are evenly coated with the dressing and mint leaves.

5. **Chill and Serve:**

- For best results, cover the bowl with plastic wrap and refrigerate the salad for at least 30 minutes to allow the flavors to meld.
- Before serving, give the salad a gentle toss and sprinkle it with a pinch of salt if desired.

6. **Serve:**

- Transfer the Minty Melon Salad to a serving platter or bowl.
- Garnish with a few additional whole mint leaves for a beautiful presentation.

Papaya and Jicama Salad

Ingredients:

- 1 medium papaya, peeled, seeded, and julienned
- 1 medium jicama, peeled and julienned
- 2 limes, juiced
- 1 teaspoon chili powder
- 1 tablespoon honey or agave syrup (optional)
- Salt to taste
- Fresh cilantro leaves, for garnish (optional)

1. **Prepare the Papaya:**

- Peel the papaya, cut it in half, and remove the seeds.
- Julienne the papaya into thin, matchstick-sized pieces.
- Place the julienned papaya in a large mixing bowl.

2. **Prepare the Jicama:**

- Peel the jicama and cut it into thin, matchstick-sized pieces.
- Add the julienned jicama to the bowl with the papaya.

3. **Make the Dressing:**

- In a small bowl, whisk together the lime juice, chili powder, honey (if using), and a pinch of salt until well combined.

4. **Combine the Ingredients:**

- Pour the dressing over the julienned papaya and jicama.
- Toss gently to coat the ingredients evenly with the dressing.

5. **Season and Adjust:**

- Taste the salad and adjust the seasoning with more salt or lime juice if needed.
- If you prefer a sweeter salad, add a bit more honey or agave syrup.

6. **Chill and Serve:**

- Cover the bowl with plastic wrap and refrigerate the salad for at least 20-30 minutes to allow the flavors to meld and to chill the salad.

7. **Garnish and Serve:**

- Before serving, give the salad a gentle toss.
- Transfer the salad to a serving platter or bowl.
- Garnish with fresh cilantro leaves if desired.

Shrimp and Mango Ceviche

Ingredients:

- 1 pound fresh shrimp, peeled and deveined
- 1 cup fresh lime juice (about 8-10 limes)
- 1 large mango, peeled and diced
- 1/2 red onion, finely diced
- 1 jalapeño, finely chopped (seeds removed for less heat)
- 1/4 cup fresh cilantro, chopped
- Salt to taste
- Freshly ground black pepper to taste
- 1 avocado, diced (optional)
- Tortilla chips, for serving

1. **Prepare the Shrimp:**

- If using raw shrimp, bring a pot of water to a boil. Add the shrimp and cook for about 2-3 minutes until they turn pink and opaque. Immediately transfer the shrimp to an ice bath to stop the cooking process. Drain and chop the shrimp into bite-sized pieces.
- If using pre-cooked shrimp, simply chop them into bite-sized pieces.

2. **Marinate the Shrimp:**

- Place the chopped shrimp in a large bowl.
- Pour the fresh lime juice over the shrimp, ensuring they are fully submerged.
- Cover the bowl with plastic wrap and refrigerate for at least 30 minutes to 1 hour, or until the shrimp are fully "cooked" by the lime juice and are opaque.

3. **Prepare the Other Ingredients:**

- While the shrimp is marinating, peel and dice the mango, finely dice the red onion, and chop the jalapeño and cilantro.

4. **Combine the Ingredients:**

- After the shrimp has marinated, drain most of the lime juice, leaving a little for flavor.
- Add the diced mango, red onion, jalapeño, and cilantro to the bowl with the shrimp.
- Gently toss to combine all the ingredients.

5. **Season and Adjust:**

- Season the ceviche with salt and freshly ground black pepper to taste.
- If using, gently fold in the diced avocado for added creaminess.

6. **Chill and Serve:**

- Cover the ceviche and refrigerate for an additional 15-20 minutes to allow the flavors to meld together.
- Serve the Shrimp and Mango Ceviche chilled, with tortilla chips on the side for scooping.

Chilled Cucumber and Melon Gazpacho

Ingredients:

- 2 large cucumbers, peeled and seeded
- 2 cups cantaloupe or honeydew melon, cubed
- 1/4 cup fresh mint leaves
- 2 tablespoons fresh lime juice (about 1-2 limes)
- 1/4 cup Greek yogurt (optional, for creaminess)
- 1/4 cup cold water (adjust for desired consistency)
- Salt to taste
- Freshly ground black pepper to taste
- Mint leaves or cucumber slices, for garnish

1. **Prepare the Ingredients:**

- Peel and seed the cucumbers. Cut them into chunks.
- Cut the melon into cubes, removing the rind and seeds.
- Juice the limes to obtain 2 tablespoons of fresh lime juice.
- Roughly chop the fresh mint leaves.

2. **Blend the Gazpacho:**

- In a blender or food processor, combine the cucumber chunks, melon cubes, chopped mint leaves, and lime juice.
- If using, add the Greek yogurt for a creamier texture.
- Add the cold water to help with blending and to achieve the desired consistency.

3. **Blend Until Smooth:**

- Blend the mixture on high until it is smooth and well combined. You may need to stop and scrape down the sides of the blender to ensure all the ingredients are incorporated.

4. **Season and Adjust:**

- Taste the gazpacho and season with salt and freshly ground black pepper to taste.
- If the gazpacho is too thick, add a bit more cold water until you reach your preferred consistency.

5. **Chill the Gazpacho:**

- Transfer the gazpacho to a large bowl or container.
- Cover and refrigerate for at least 1-2 hours, or until well chilled. Chilling allows the flavors to meld and enhances the refreshing quality of the soup.

6. **Serve:**

- Before serving, give the gazpacho a quick stir.
- Ladle the chilled gazpacho into bowls.
- Garnish with fresh mint leaves or cucumber slices for an added touch of freshness.

Tomato and Watermelon Gazpacho

Ingredients:

- 4 cups ripe tomatoes, chopped
- 2 cups watermelon, seeded and cubed
- 1 cucumber, peeled and chopped
- 1/2 red bell pepper, chopped
- 1/2 red onion, chopped
- 2 cloves garlic, minced
- 1/4 cup fresh basil leaves, chopped
- 2 tablespoons red wine vinegar
- 2 tablespoons extra virgin olive oil
- Salt to taste
- Freshly ground black pepper to taste
- Fresh basil leaves, for garnish

1. **Prepare the Ingredients:**

- Chop the tomatoes into chunks.
- Seed and cube the watermelon.
- Peel and chop the cucumber.
- Chop the red bell pepper and red onion.
- Mince the garlic.

- Roughly chop the fresh basil leaves.

2. **Blend the Gazpacho:**

- In a blender or food processor, combine the chopped tomatoes, watermelon, cucumber, red bell pepper, red onion, minced garlic, and chopped basil leaves.
- Blend on high until the mixture is smooth and well combined.

3. **Add the Seasonings:**

- Add the red wine vinegar and extra virgin olive oil to the blender.
- Season with salt and freshly ground black pepper to taste.
- Blend again to fully incorporate the seasonings.

4. **Adjust Consistency:**

- If the gazpacho is too thick, you can add a little cold water to achieve your desired consistency. Blend until smooth.

5. **Chill the Gazpacho:**

- Transfer the gazpacho to a large bowl or container.
- Cover and refrigerate for at least 1-2 hours, or until well chilled. Chilling enhances the flavors and refreshing quality of the soup.

6. **Serve:**

- Before serving, give the gazpacho a good stir.
- Ladle the chilled gazpacho into bowls.
- Garnish with fresh basil leaves for a touch of color and added flavor.

Chilled Avocado and Cucumber Soup

Ingredients:

- 2 large ripe avocados
- 2 large cucumbers, peeled and seeded
- 1 cup plain Greek yogurt
- 1/2 cup cold water (adjust for desired consistency)
- 2 tablespoons fresh lime juice (about 1-2 limes)
- 1 garlic clove, minced
- 1/4 cup fresh cilantro leaves, chopped
- Salt to taste
- Freshly ground black pepper to taste
- Optional: a few dashes of hot sauce
- Optional: extra virgin olive oil, for drizzling
- Garnish: thin cucumber slices, avocado slices, cilantro leaves, or a dollop of Greek yogurt

1. **Prepare the Ingredients:**

- Peel and seed the cucumbers. Cut them into chunks.
- Cut the avocados in half, remove the pits, and scoop the flesh into a blender or food processor.

2. **Blend the Soup:**

- In the blender or food processor, combine the cucumber chunks, avocado flesh, Greek yogurt, cold water, fresh lime juice, minced garlic, and chopped cilantro leaves.
- Blend on high until the mixture is smooth and creamy.

3. **Season the Soup:**

- Taste the soup and season with salt and freshly ground black pepper to taste.
- If desired, add a few dashes of hot sauce for a hint of heat.
- Blend again to fully incorporate the seasonings.

4. **Adjust Consistency:**

- If the soup is too thick, add a bit more cold water and blend until you reach your preferred consistency.

5. **Chill the Soup:**

- Transfer the soup to a large bowl or container.
- Cover and refrigerate for at least 1-2 hours, or until well chilled. Chilling enhances the flavors and makes the soup more refreshing.

6. **Serve:**

- Before serving, give the soup a good stir.
- Ladle the chilled soup into bowls.
- Garnish with thin cucumber slices, avocado slices, cilantro leaves, or a dollop of Greek yogurt.
- For an extra touch, drizzle a small amount of extra virgin olive oil on top.

Tropical Fruit Platter with Lime-Yogurt Dip

Ingredients:

For the Fruit Platter:

- 1 pineapple, peeled, cored, and sliced
- 2 mangoes, peeled and sliced
- 4 kiwis, peeled and sliced
- 1 papaya, peeled, seeded, and sliced
- 1/2 cup fresh strawberries, hulled and halved (optional for color and variety)
- Fresh mint leaves, for garnish

For the Lime-Yogurt Dip:

- 1 cup plain Greek yogurt
- 2 tablespoons honey or agave syrup
- 2 tablespoons fresh lime juice (about 1-2 limes)
- 1 teaspoon lime zest

1. **Prepare the Fruits:**

- Pineapple: Cut off the top and bottom of the pineapple, then slice off the skin. Cut the pineapple into rings or wedges, removing the core.
- Mangoes: Peel the mangoes and slice the flesh away from the pit. Cut the mango flesh into slices or cubes.
- Kiwis: Peel the kiwis and slice them into rounds.
- Papaya: Peel the papaya, cut it in half, and remove the seeds. Slice the papaya into strips or cubes.
- Strawberries: If using, hull and halve the strawberries.

2. **Assemble the Fruit Platter:**

- Arrange the pineapple, mango, kiwi, papaya, and strawberries (if using) on a large serving platter. Create an aesthetically pleasing arrangement by alternating colors and shapes.
- Garnish with fresh mint leaves for a pop of color and added freshness.

3. **Prepare the Lime-Yogurt Dip:**

- In a small bowl, combine the plain Greek yogurt, honey or agave syrup, fresh lime juice, and lime zest.
- Stir until well combined and smooth.
- Transfer the dip to a small serving bowl and place it in the center of the fruit platter or alongside it.

4. **Serve:**

- Serve the tropical fruit platter immediately with the lime-yogurt dip on the side.
- Encourage guests to dip the fruit slices into the tangy and sweet lime-yogurt dip for a refreshing treat.

Lemon Basil Pasta Salad

Ingredients:

For the Salad:

- 12 ounces pasta (such as penne, fusilli, or farfalle)
- 1 pint cherry tomatoes, halved
- 8 ounces mozzarella balls
- (bocconcini), halved if large
- 1/2 cup fresh basil leaves, chopped
- 1/4 cup red onion, thinly sliced (optional)

For the Lemon-Basil Vinaigrette:

- 1/4 cup fresh lemon juice (about 2 lemons)
- 1 tablespoon lemon zest (from 1 lemon)
- 1/4 cup extra virgin olive oil
- 1 tablespoon Dijon mustard
- 1 tablespoon honey or agave syrup
- 1 clove garlic, minced
- 1/4 cup fresh basil leaves, finely chopped
- Salt and freshly ground black pepper to taste

1. **Cook the Pasta:**

- Bring a large pot of salted water to a boil.
- Add the pasta and cook according to the package instructions until al dente.
- Drain the pasta and rinse under cold water to stop the cooking process.
- Set aside.

2. **Prepare the Lemon-Basil Vinaigrette:**

- In a small bowl, whisk together the fresh lemon juice, lemon zest, extra virgin olive oil, Dijon mustard, honey, and minced garlic until well combined.
- Stir in the finely chopped fresh basil leaves.
- Season with salt and freshly ground black pepper to taste.
- Adjust the sweetness or acidity by adding more honey or lemon juice as needed.

3. **Assemble the Salad:**

- In a large salad bowl, combine the cooked and cooled pasta, halved cherry tomatoes, mozzarella balls, chopped fresh basil, and thinly sliced red onion (if using).
- Pour the lemon-basil vinaigrette over the pasta salad.

4. **Toss and Chill:**

- Gently toss the salad until all the ingredients are evenly coated with the vinaigrette.
- Cover and refrigerate for at least 30 minutes to allow the flavors to meld and the salad to chill.

5. **Serve:**

- Before serving, give the salad a gentle toss to redistribute the vinaigrette.
- Garnish with additional fresh basil leaves if desired.
- Serve the Lemon Basil Pasta Salad cold or at room temperature.

Chilled Quinoa Salad with Summer Veggies

Ingredients:

For the Salad:

- 1 cup quinoa
- 2 cups water
- 1 cucumber, diced
- 1 pint cherry tomatoes, halved
- 1 red bell pepper, diced
- 1 yellow bell pepper, diced
- 1/4 cup red onion, finely diced
- 1/4 cup fresh parsley, chopped
- 1/4 cup fresh mint, chopped (optional)

For the Lemon-Tahini Dressing:

- 1/4 cup tahini
- 1/4 cup fresh lemon juice (about 2 lemons)
- 2 tablespoons extra virgin olive oil
- 1 tablespoon honey or maple syrup
- 1 clove garlic, minced
- 1/4 teaspoon ground cumin

- Salt and freshly ground black pepper to taste
- 2-4 tablespoons water (to thin the dressing to desired consistency)

1. **Cook the Quinoa:**

- Rinse the quinoa under cold water to remove any bitterness.
- In a medium saucepan, combine the quinoa and water. Bring to a boil over medium-high heat.
- Reduce the heat to low, cover, and simmer for about 15 minutes, or until the quinoa is tender and the water is absorbed.
- Remove from heat and let it sit, covered, for 5 minutes. Fluff with a fork and transfer to a large mixing bowl to cool completely.

2. **Prepare the Lemon-Tahini Dressing:**

- In a small bowl, whisk together the tahini, fresh lemon juice, extra virgin olive oil, honey or maple syrup, minced garlic, and ground cumin.
- Season with salt and freshly ground black pepper to taste.
- Add water, 1 tablespoon at a time, until the dressing reaches your desired consistency (smooth and pourable).

3. **Prepare the Summer Veggies:**

- While the quinoa is cooling, dice the cucumber, halve the cherry tomatoes, and dice the red and yellow bell peppers.
- Finely dice the red onion and chop the fresh parsley and mint (if using).

4. **Assemble the Salad:**

- Once the quinoa is completely cooled, add the diced cucumber, cherry tomatoes, red and yellow bell peppers, red onion, fresh parsley, and mint (if using) to the bowl with the quinoa.
- Pour the lemon-tahini dressing over the salad.

5. **Toss and Chill:**

- Gently toss the salad until all the ingredients are evenly coated with the dressing.
- Cover and refrigerate for at least 30 minutes to allow the flavors to meld and the salad to chill.

6. **Serve:**

- Before serving, give the salad a gentle toss to redistribute the dressing.
- Garnish with additional chopped parsley or mint if desired.
- Serve the Chilled Quinoa Salad with Summer Veggies cold.

Strawberry Spinach Salad with Poppy Seed Dressing

Ingredients:

For the Salad:

- 6 cups fresh spinach leaves, washed and dried
- 1 pint strawberries, hulled and sliced
- 1/2 cup sliced almonds, toasted
- 1/4 red onion, thinly sliced (optional)
- 1/4 cup crumbled feta cheese (optional)

For the Poppy Seed Dressing:

- 1/4 cup extra virgin olive oil
- 2 tablespoons apple cider vinegar
- 2 tablespoons honey or maple syrup
- 1 tablespoon poppy seeds
- 1 teaspoon Dijon mustard
- 1/2 teaspoon salt
- Freshly ground black pepper to taste

1. **Prepare the Poppy Seed Dressing:**

- In a small bowl or a jar with a lid, combine the extra virgin olive oil, apple cider vinegar, honey or maple syrup, poppy seeds, Dijon mustard, salt, and freshly ground black pepper.
- Whisk or shake well until the dressing is well combined and emulsified.
- Taste and adjust the seasoning if needed. Set aside.

2. **Prepare the Salad Ingredients:**

- Wash and dry the fresh spinach leaves.
- Hull and slice the strawberries.
- Toast the sliced almonds in a dry skillet over medium heat, stirring frequently, until golden brown and fragrant. Remove from heat and let cool.

3. **Assemble the Salad:**

- In a large salad bowl, combine the fresh spinach leaves, sliced strawberries, toasted almonds, and thinly sliced red onion (if using).
- If desired, add crumbled feta cheese for extra flavor.

4. **Dress the Salad:**

- Just before serving, drizzle the poppy seed dressing over the salad.
- Gently toss to coat the ingredients evenly with the dressing.

5. **Serve:**

- Transfer the Strawberry Spinach Salad to a serving platter or individual plates.
- Serve immediately.

Spicy Grilled Corn on the Cob

Ingredients:

For the Corn:

- 6 ears of corn, husked
- 2 tablespoons olive oil

For the Spicy Lime Butter:

- 1/2 cup unsalted butter, softened
- 1 tablespoon lime juice (about 1 lime)
- 1 teaspoon lime zest (from 1 lime)
- 1 teaspoon chili powder
- 1/2 teaspoon smoked paprika
- 1/4 teaspoon cayenne pepper (adjust to taste)
- 1 clove garlic, minced
- Salt and freshly ground black pepper to taste

For Garnish:

- 1/2 cup crumbled cotija cheese
- 1/4 cup fresh cilantro, chopped

- Lime wedges (optional)

1. **Prepare the Spicy Lime Butter:**

- In a small bowl, combine the softened butter, lime juice, lime zest, chili powder, smoked paprika, cayenne pepper, minced garlic, salt, and freshly ground black pepper.
- Mix well until all ingredients are thoroughly incorporated.
- Set aside.

2. **Prepare the Corn:**

- Preheat your grill to medium-high heat (about 375-400°F).
- Lightly brush the husked ears of corn with olive oil to prevent sticking.
- Season the corn with a little salt and pepper.

3. **Grill the Corn:**

- Place the ears of corn on the preheated grill.
- Grill the corn for about 10-12 minutes, turning every 2-3 minutes, until the corn is tender and charred in spots.
- Remove the corn from the grill and set aside.

4. **Apply the Spicy Lime Butter:**

- While the corn is still hot, generously brush each ear with the spicy lime butter.
- Let the butter melt and soak into the corn.

5. **Garnish the Corn:**

- Sprinkle the crumbled cotija cheese evenly over the buttered corn.
- Garnish with chopped fresh cilantro.
- Serve with lime wedges on the side for squeezing over the corn (optional).

6. **Serve:**

- Transfer the Spicy Grilled Corn on the Cob to a serving platter.
- Serve immediately while hot.

Grilled Veggie Skewers

Ingredients:

For the Vegetables:

- 2 medium zucchinis, sliced into 1/2-inch rounds
- 2 red bell peppers, cut into 1-inch pieces
- 2 yellow bell peppers, cut into 1-inch pieces
- 1 pint cherry tomatoes
- 8 ounces mushrooms, halved if large
- Wooden or metal skewers (if using wooden skewers, soak them in water for at least 30 minutes to prevent burning)

For the Marinade:

- 1/4 cup olive oil
- 3 tablespoons balsamic vinegar
- 2 tablespoons soy sauce
- 2 tablespoons lemon juice (about 1 lemon)
- 2 cloves garlic, minced
- 1 teaspoon dried oregano
- 1 teaspoon dried basil

- 1/2 teaspoon dried thyme
- 1/2 teaspoon smoked paprika
- Salt and freshly ground black pepper to taste

1. **Prepare the Marinade:**

- In a small bowl, whisk together the olive oil, balsamic vinegar, soy sauce, lemon juice, minced garlic, dried oregano, dried basil, dried thyme, smoked paprika, salt, and freshly ground black pepper until well combined.

2. **Marinate the Vegetables:**

- Place the zucchini rounds, bell pepper pieces, cherry tomatoes, and mushroom halves in a large resealable plastic bag or a shallow dish.
- Pour the marinade over the vegetables, ensuring they are evenly coated.
- Seal the bag or cover the dish and refrigerate for at least 30 minutes to 1 hour, turning occasionally to evenly marinate the vegetables.

3. **Preheat the Grill:**

- Preheat your grill to medium-high heat (about 375-400°F).
- Lightly oil the grill grates to prevent sticking.

4. **Prepare the Skewers:**

- If using wooden skewers, soak them in water for at least 30 minutes to prevent burning.
- Thread the marinated vegetables onto the skewers, alternating between zucchini, bell peppers, cherry tomatoes, and mushrooms for a colorful presentation.

5. **Grill the Veggie Skewers:**

- Place the veggie skewers on the preheated grill.
- Grill for about 10-12 minutes, turning every 2-3 minutes, until the vegetables are tender and have nice grill marks.
- Baste with any remaining marinade during grilling for extra flavor.

6. **Serve:**

- Transfer the Grilled Veggie Skewers to a serving platter.
- Serve immediately as a delicious side dish or a light vegetarian main course.

Fresh Berry and Spinach Salad

Ingredients:

For the Salad:

- 6 cups fresh spinach leaves, washed and dried
- 1 cup strawberries, hulled and sliced
- 1 cup blueberries
- 1 cup raspberries
- 1/2 cup goat cheese, crumbled
- 1/4 cup sliced almonds, toasted (optional)

For the Raspberry Vinaigrette:

- 1/2 cup fresh raspberries
- 1/4 cup olive oil
- 2 tablespoons apple cider vinegar
- 1 tablespoon honey or maple syrup
- 1 teaspoon Dijon mustard
- Salt and freshly ground black pepper to taste

1. **Prepare the Raspberry Vinaigrette:**

- In a blender or food processor, combine the fresh raspberries, olive oil, apple cider vinegar, honey, Dijon mustard, salt, and freshly ground black pepper.
- Blend until smooth and well combined.
- Taste and adjust the seasoning if needed.
- Set aside.

2. **Prepare the Salad Ingredients:**

- Wash and dry the fresh spinach leaves.
- Hull and slice the strawberries.
- Toast the sliced almonds in a dry skillet over medium heat, stirring frequently, until golden brown and fragrant. Remove from heat and let cool.

3. **Assemble the Salad:**

- In a large salad bowl, combine the fresh spinach leaves, sliced strawberries, blueberries, and raspberries.
- Add the crumbled goat cheese and toasted sliced almonds (if using).

4. **Dress the Salad:**

- Just before serving, drizzle the raspberry vinaigrette over the salad.
- Gently toss to coat the ingredients evenly with the dressing.

5. **Serve:**

- Transfer the Fresh Berry and Spinach Salad to a serving platter or individual plates.
- Serve immediately.

Chilled Orzo and Vegetable Salad

Ingredients:

For the Salad:

- 1 1/2 cups orzo pasta
- 1 large cucumber, diced
- 1 pint cherry tomatoes, halved
- 1/2 cup Kalamata olives, pitted and sliced
- 1/4 cup red onion, finely diced
- 1/4 cup crumbled feta cheese (optional)
- 1/4 cup fresh dill, chopped

For the Lemon-Dill Dressing:

- 1/4 cup fresh lemon juice (about 2 lemons)
- 1 tablespoon lemon zest (from 1 lemon)
- 1/4 cup extra virgin olive oil
- 1 tablespoon Dijon mustard
- 1 tablespoon honey or maple syrup
- 2 cloves garlic, minced
- 1/4 cup fresh dill, finely chopped
- Salt and freshly ground black pepper to taste

1. **Cook the Orzo:**

- Bring a large pot of salted water to a boil.
- Add the orzo pasta and cook according to the package instructions until al dente.
- Drain the orzo and rinse under cold water to stop the cooking process.
- Transfer the cooked orzo to a large mixing bowl and let it cool completely.

2. **Prepare the Lemon-Dill Dressing:**

- In a small bowl, whisk together the fresh lemon juice, lemon zest, extra virgin olive oil, Dijon mustard, honey, and minced garlic until well combined.
- Stir in the finely chopped fresh dill.
- Season with salt and freshly ground black pepper to taste.
- Adjust the sweetness or acidity by adding more honey or lemon juice as needed.

3. **Prepare the Vegetables:**

- Dice the cucumber.
- Halve the cherry tomatoes.
- Pit and slice the Kalamata olives.
- Finely dice the red onion.
- Chop the fresh dill.

4. **Assemble the Salad:**

- Once the orzo is completely cooled, add the diced cucumber, halved cherry tomatoes, sliced olives, finely diced red onion, and crumbled feta cheese (if using) to the bowl with the orzo.
- Pour the lemon-dill dressing over the salad.

5. **Toss and Chill:**

- Gently toss the salad until all the ingredients are evenly coated with the dressing.
- Cover and refrigerate for at least 30 minutes to allow the flavors to meld and the salad to chill.

6. **Serve:**

- Before serving, give the salad a gentle toss to redistribute the dressing.
- Garnish with additional fresh dill if desired.
- Serve the Chilled Orzo and Vegetable Salad cold.

Tropical Chicken Salad
For the Salad:

Ingredients:

For the Salad:

- 2 cups cooked and shredded chicken breast (about 2-3 chicken breasts)
- 1 cup fresh pineapple, diced
- 1 red bell pepper, diced
- 3 green onions, thinly sliced
- 1/4 cup fresh cilantro, chopped (optional)
- 1/4 cup sliced almonds, toasted (optional)

For the Light Curry Dressing:

- 1/2 cup plain Greek yogurt
- 1/4 cup mayonnaise
- 1 tablespoon curry powder
- 1 tablespoon honey or maple syrup
- 1 tablespoon fresh lime juice (about 1 lime)
- 1 teaspoon lime zest (from 1 lime)
- Salt and freshly ground black pepper to taste

1. **Cook and Shred the Chicken:**

- If not using pre-cooked chicken, cook the chicken breasts by boiling, baking, or grilling until fully cooked.
- Allow the chicken to cool, then shred it into bite-sized pieces using two forks.

2. **Prepare the Light Curry Dressing:**

- In a small bowl, whisk together the plain Greek yogurt, mayonnaise, curry powder, honey, fresh lime juice, and lime zest until well combined.
- Season with salt and freshly ground black pepper to taste.
- Adjust the sweetness or acidity by adding more honey or lime juice as needed.

3. **Prepare the Salad Ingredients:**

- Dice the fresh pineapple.
- Dice the red bell pepper.
- Thinly slice the green onions.
- Chop the fresh cilantro, if using.
- Toast the sliced almonds in a dry skillet over medium heat, stirring frequently, until golden brown and fragrant. Remove from heat and let cool.

4. **Assemble the Salad:**

- In a large salad bowl, combine the shredded chicken, diced pineapple, diced red bell pepper, and sliced green onions.
- If using, add the chopped fresh cilantro and toasted sliced almonds.

5. **Add the Dressing:**

- Pour the light curry dressing over the salad ingredients.
- Gently toss the salad until all the ingredients are evenly coated with the dressing.

6. **Chill and Serve:**

- Cover and refrigerate the Tropical Chicken Salad for at least 30 minutes to allow the flavors to meld and the salad to chill.
- Before serving, give the salad a gentle toss to redistribute the dressing.
- Garnish with additional fresh cilantro or toasted almonds if desired.

7. **Serve:**

- Serve the Tropical Chicken Salad on a bed of lettuce, in a sandwich, or with crackers for a refreshing and flavorful meal.

Citrus Avocado Shrimp Salad

Ingredients:

For the Salad:

- 1 pound large shrimp, peeled and deveined
- 1 tablespoon olive oil
- 1 teaspoon paprika
- Salt and freshly ground black pepper to taste
- 6 cups mixed fresh greens (such as arugula, baby spinach, and romaine)
- 1 large avocado, peeled, pitted, and sliced
- 2 grapefruits, segmented
- 1/2 red onion, thinly sliced
- 1/4 cup fresh cilantro, chopped (optional)

For the Citrus Vinaigrette:

- 1/4 cup fresh orange juice (about 1 orange)
- 2 tablespoons fresh grapefruit juice (from segmented grapefruit)
- 2 tablespoons fresh lime juice (about 1 lime)
- 1/4 cup olive oil
- 1 tablespoon honey or agave syrup
- 1 teaspoon Dijon mustard

- Salt and freshly ground black pepper to taste

1. **Prepare the Shrimp:**

- In a medium bowl, toss the shrimp with olive oil, paprika, salt, and freshly ground black pepper.
- Preheat your grill or grill pan to medium-high heat.
- Grill the shrimp for about 2-3 minutes per side, or until they are pink and opaque.
- Remove from the grill and set aside to cool slightly.

2. **Prepare the Citrus Vinaigrette:**

- In a small bowl, whisk together the fresh orange juice, grapefruit juice, lime juice, olive oil, honey, and Dijon mustard until well combined.
- Season with salt and freshly ground black pepper to taste.
- Adjust the sweetness or acidity by adding more honey or citrus juice as needed.

3. **Prepare the Salad Ingredients:**

- Wash and dry the mixed greens.
- Peel, pit, and slice the avocado.
- Segment the grapefruits, reserving 2 tablespoons of juice for the vinaigrette.
- Thinly slice the red onion.
- Chop the fresh cilantro, if using.

4. **Assemble the Salad:**

- In a large salad bowl, combine the mixed greens, sliced avocado, grapefruit segments, sliced red onion, and chopped cilantro.
- Add the grilled shrimp to the salad.

5. **Add the Dressing:**

- Pour the citrus vinaigrette over the salad ingredients.
- Gently toss the salad until all the ingredients are evenly coated with the dressing.

6. **Serve:**

- Transfer the Citrus Avocado Shrimp Salad to a serving platter or individual plates.
- Serve immediately.

MAIN DISHES

SUMMER

Filipino Chicken Adobo
Jemmalyn's Favorite!

Ingredients

- ¾ cup vinegar
- ¾ cup light or low-sodium soy sauce
- 1 teaspoon whole black peppercorns
- 2 ½ pounds boneless, skinless chicken thighs
- 2 tablespoons neutral oil (such as avocado oil), divided
- 1 medium yellow onion, thinly sliced
- 5 cloves garlic, thinly sliced or minced
- 3 bay leaves (fresh preferred, or dried if unavailable)
- 2 teaspoons brown sugar (or white sugar)
- 4 green onions, thinly sliced (for garnish)
- White rice, for serving

1. In a large bowl, combine the vinegar, soy sauce, and peppercorns. Add the chicken thighs and marinate for at least 20 minutes, or up to overnight.

2. Heat 1 tablespoon oil over high heat in a large skillet or pot. Remove chicken from marinade, allowing excess to drip back into the bowl (reserve marinade). Place chicken smooth side down in the hot pan.

Cook undisturbed for 2–3 minutes until golden, then flip and cook for 2 minutes more. Transfer chicken to a plate.

3. Reduce heat to medium-low and add the remaining 1 tablespoon oil. Add onion and garlic, cooking until fragrant and slightly browned, about 2 minutes.

4. Add the reserved marinade, bay leaves, and sugar. Bring to a rolling boil, then reduce to medium and simmer for 3–4 minutes.

5. Return the chicken thighs, smooth side down. Simmer uncovered for 10 minutes, then flip and continue to simmer for another 10–15 minutes, spooning sauce over the top, until the sauce reduces by at least half.

6. If needed, remove chicken and continue simmering sauce until glaze-like but not overly thick. Return chicken to warm through.

7. Serve immediately with white rice and extra adobo sauce. Garnish with sliced green onions.

Chef's Note

This dish holds a special place in **Jemmalyn Hewlett's heart** as one of her all-time favorites. A nod to her Filipino heritage, it's comfort food at its finest—bold, tangy, and savory. For a true Poolside Cooking™ experience, pair it with a refreshing tropical drink like our Tropical Mango Margarita or Minty Cucumber Lemonade.

Grilled Lemon Herb Shrimp Skewers

Ingredients:

- 1 pound large shrimp, peeled and deveined
- 3 tablespoons olive oil
- 2 tablespoons fresh lemon juice (about 1 lemon)
- 1 tablespoon lemon zest (from 1 lemon)
- 3 cloves garlic, minced
- 2 tablespoons fresh parsley, chopped
- 1 tablespoon fresh thyme leaves, chopped
- 1 tablespoon fresh oregano leaves, chopped
- Salt and freshly ground black pepper to taste
- Wooden or metal skewers (if using wooden skewers, soak them in water for at least 30 minutes to prevent burning)

1. **Prepare the Marinade:**

- In a large mixing bowl, combine the olive oil, fresh lemon juice, lemon zest, minced garlic, chopped parsley, thyme, and oregano.
- Season with salt and freshly ground black pepper to taste. Mix well to combine all the ingredients.

2. **Marinate the Shrimp:**

- Add the peeled and deveined shrimp to the bowl with the marinade.
- Toss the shrimp to coat them evenly with the marinade.
- Cover the bowl with plastic wrap and refrigerate for at least 30 minutes to 1 hour, allowing the shrimp to absorb the flavors.

3. **Prepare the Skewers:**

- If using wooden skewers, soak them in water for at least 30 minutes to prevent burning on the grill.
- Thread the marinated shrimp onto the skewers, piercing through the tail and the thicker part of each shrimp to ensure they lay flat on the grill.

4. **Preheat the Grill:**

- Preheat your grill to medium-high heat (about 375-400°F).

5. **Grill the Shrimp:**

- Lightly oil the grill grates to prevent sticking.
- Place the shrimp skewers on the preheated grill.
- Grill the shrimp for about 2-3 minutes per side, or until they turn pink and opaque, with nice grill marks. Be careful not to overcook the shrimp, as they can become tough and rubbery.

6. **Serve:**

- Remove the shrimp skewers from the grill and transfer them to a serving platter.
- Garnish with additional fresh herbs and lemon wedges if desired.

Mango Salsa Grilled Fish Tacos

Ingredients:

For the Grilled Fish:

- 1 pound white fish fillets (such as tilapia, cod, or mahi-mahi)
- 2 tablespoons olive oil
- 2 tablespoons fresh lime juice (about 1-2 limes)
- 2 cloves garlic, minced
- 1 teaspoon ground cumin
- 1 teaspoon smoked paprika
- Salt and freshly ground black pepper to taste

For the Mango Salsa:

- 1 large ripe mango, peeled, pitted, and diced
- 1/2 red bell pepper, diced
- 1/2 red onion, finely diced
- 1 jalapeño, finely chopped (seeds removed for less heat)
- 1/4 cup fresh cilantro, chopped
- 2 tablespoons fresh lime juice (about 1-2 limes)
- Salt to taste

For the Tacos:

- 8 small soft tortillas (corn or flour)
- Optional toppings: shredded cabbage or lettuce, sliced avocado, lime wedges, extra cilantro

1. **Prepare the Fish Marinade:**

- In a small bowl, whisk together the olive oil, fresh lime juice, minced garlic, ground cumin, smoked paprika, salt, and pepper.
- Place the fish fillets in a shallow dish and pour the marinade over them, ensuring they are evenly coated.
- Cover and refrigerate for at least 20-30 minutes to allow the flavors to meld.

2. **Prepare the Mango Salsa:**

- In a medium bowl, combine the diced mango, red bell pepper, red onion, jalapeño, and chopped cilantro.
- Add the fresh lime juice and salt to taste.
- Gently toss to combine all the ingredients.
- Cover and refrigerate until ready to use.

3. **Preheat the Grill:**

- Preheat your grill to medium-high heat (about 375-400°F).

4. **Grill the Fish:**

- Lightly oil the grill grates to prevent sticking.
- Place the marinated fish fillets on the preheated grill.
- Grill the fish for about 3-4 minutes per side, or until the fish is opaque and flakes easily with a fork.
- Remove the fish from the grill and let it rest for a few minutes. Then, gently flake the fish into bite-sized pieces.

5. **Warm the Tortillas:**

- While the fish is resting, warm the tortillas on the grill for about 20-30 seconds per side, until they are pliable and have slight grill marks.

6. **Assemble the Tacos:**

- Place a few pieces of grilled fish in the center of each tortilla.
- Top with a generous spoonful of mango salsa.
- Add any optional toppings such as shredded cabbage or lettuce, sliced avocado, extra cilantro, and a squeeze of fresh lime juice.

7. **Serve:**

- Serve the Mango Salsa Grilled Fish Tacos immediately, with extra lime wedges on the side for squeezing over the tacos.

Tropical Pineapple Chicken Kebabs

Ingredients:

For the Marinade:

- 1/2 cup soy sauce
- 1/4 cup pineapple juice
- 1/4 cup brown sugar
- 2 tablespoons honey
- 2 tablespoons rice vinegar
- 2 cloves garlic, minced
- 1 tablespoon fresh ginger, grated
- 1 tablespoon sesame oil
- 1/4 teaspoon black pepper

For the Kebabs:

- 1 1/2 pounds boneless, skinless chicken breasts or thighs, cut into 1-inch cubes
- 1 fresh pineapple, peeled, cored, and cut into 1-inch cubes
- 2 red bell peppers, cut into 1-inch pieces
- 1 large red onion, cut into 1-inch pieces

- Wooden or metal skewers (if using wooden skewers, soak them in water for at least 30 minutes to prevent burning)

1. **Prepare the Marinade:**

- In a medium bowl, whisk together the soy sauce, pineapple juice, brown sugar, honey, rice vinegar, minced garlic, grated ginger, sesame oil, and black pepper until well combined.

2. **Marinate the Chicken:**

- Place the cubed chicken in a large resealable plastic bag or a shallow dish.
- Pour half of the marinade over the chicken, reserving the other half for basting and serving.
- Seal the bag or cover the dish and refrigerate for at least 1 hour, preferably 2-3 hours, to allow the flavors to meld.

3. **Prepare the Skewers:**

- Preheat your grill to medium-high heat (about 375-400°F).
- Thread the marinated chicken, pineapple cubes, red bell pepper pieces, and red onion pieces alternately onto the skewers.

4. **Grill the Kebabs:**

- Lightly oil the grill grates to prevent sticking.
- Place the kebabs on the preheated grill.
- Grill the kebabs for about 10-12 minutes, turning occasionally and basting with the reserved marinade, until the chicken is cooked through and has nice grill marks.

5. **Serve:**

- Remove the kebabs from the grill and transfer them to a serving platter.
- Drizzle any remaining reserved marinade over the kebabs, or serve it on the side as a dipping sauce.

Grilled Pineapple Teriyaki Salmon

Ingredients:

For the Teriyaki Marinade:

- 1/2 cup soy sauce
- 1/4 cup pineapple juice
- 1/4 cup brown sugar
- 2 tablespoons honey
- 2 tablespoons rice vinegar
- 2 cloves garlic, minced
- 1 tablespoon fresh ginger, grated
- 1 tablespoon sesame oil
- 1/4 teaspoon black pepper

For the Salmon:

- 4 salmon fillets (about 6 ounces each), skin removed
- 8 pineapple rings (fresh or canned)
- 1 tablespoon olive oil
- 2 green onions, thinly sliced (for garnish)
- Sesame seeds (for garnish)

1. **Prepare the Teriyaki Marinade:**

- In a medium bowl, whisk together the soy sauce, pineapple juice, brown sugar, honey, rice vinegar, minced garlic, grated ginger, sesame oil, and black pepper until well combined.

2. **Marinate the Salmon:**

- Place the salmon fillets in a large resealable plastic bag or a shallow dish.
- Pour the teriyaki marinade over the salmon, ensuring each fillet is well coated.
- Seal the bag or cover the dish and refrigerate for at least 30 minutes, up to 2 hours.

3. **Preheat the Grill:**

- Preheat your grill to medium-high heat (about 375-400°F).
- Lightly oil the grill grates to prevent sticking.

4. **Grill the Salmon and Pineapple:**

- Remove the salmon fillets from the marinade, letting the excess marinade drip off.
- Place the salmon fillets on the preheated grill.
- Grill the salmon for about 4-5 minutes per side, or until the fish is opaque and flakes easily with a fork.
- While the salmon is grilling, brush the pineapple rings with a bit of olive oil and place them on the grill.
- Grill the pineapple rings for 2-3 minutes per side, or until they are caramelized and have nice grill marks.

5. **Serve:**

- Transfer the grilled salmon fillets to a serving platter.
- Place two grilled pineapple rings on top of each salmon fillet.
- Garnish with thinly sliced green onions and a sprinkle of sesame seeds.

Coconut Lime Shrimp Lettuce Wraps

Ingredients:

For the Shrimp:

- 1 pound large shrimp, peeled and deveined
- 1 tablespoon olive oil
- 1/2 cup coconut milk
- 2 tablespoons fresh lime juice (about 1-2 limes)
- 1 tablespoon lime zest (from 1 lime)
- 2 cloves garlic, minced
- 1 tablespoon fresh ginger, grated
- 1 tablespoon fish sauce (optional)
- 1 tablespoon soy sauce
- 1 teaspoon honey or agave syrup
- 1/4 teaspoon red pepper flakes (optional, for heat)
- Salt and freshly ground black pepper to taste

For the Lettuce Wraps:

- 1 head butter lettuce or romaine lettuce, leaves separated and washed
- 1/2 cup shredded carrots

- 1/2 cup red bell pepper, thinly sliced
- 1/4 cup fresh cilantro leaves, chopped
- 1/4 cup green onions, thinly sliced
- Lime wedges, for garnish

1. **Prepare the Shrimp:**

- In a large skillet, heat the olive oil over medium-high heat.
- Add the minced garlic and grated ginger to the skillet and sauté for about 1 minute, until fragrant.
- Add the shrimp to the skillet and cook for about 2-3 minutes per side, until they turn pink and opaque.

2. **Make the Coconut Lime Sauce:**

- Reduce the heat to medium and pour the coconut milk into the skillet with the shrimp.
- Add the fresh lime juice, lime zest, fish sauce (if using), soy sauce, honey, and red pepper flakes (if using).
- Stir to combine all the ingredients and bring the sauce to a gentle simmer.
- Cook for an additional 2-3 minutes, until the shrimp are fully cooked and the sauce has slightly thickened.
- Season with salt and freshly ground black pepper to taste.

3. **Prepare the Lettuce Wraps:**

- Separate the lettuce leaves and wash them thoroughly. Pat them dry with a paper towel.
- Arrange the lettuce leaves on a large serving platter.

4. **Assemble the Lettuce Wraps:**

- Spoon the coconut lime shrimp mixture onto the center of each lettuce leaf.
- Top with shredded carrots, thinly sliced red bell pepper, chopped cilantro, and sliced green onions.

5. **Serve:**

- Garnish the lettuce wraps with lime wedges for squeezing over the top.
- Serve the Coconut Lime Shrimp Lettuce Wraps immediately as a light and refreshing poolside appetizer or main dish.

Grilled Tuna with Pineapple Salsa

Ingredients:

For the Tuna:

- 4 tuna steaks (about 6 ounces each)
- 2 tablespoons olive oil
- 2 tablespoons fresh lime juice (about 1-2 limes)
- 2 cloves garlic, minced
- Salt and freshly ground black pepper to taste

For the Pineapple Salsa:

- 1 1/2 cups fresh pineapple, diced
- 1/2 red bell pepper, diced
- 1/4 red onion, finely diced
- jalapeño, finely chopped (seeds removed for less heat)
- 1/4 cup fresh cilantro, chopped
- 2 tablespoons fresh lime juice (about 1-2 limes)
- Salt to taste

1. **Prepare the Tuna Marinade:**

- In a small bowl, whisk together the olive oil, fresh lime juice, and minced garlic.
- Season the tuna steaks with salt and freshly ground black pepper on both sides.
- Place the tuna steaks in a shallow dish and pour the marinade over them, ensuring they are evenly coated.
- Cover and refrigerate for at least 20-30 minutes.

2. **Prepare the Pineapple Salsa:**

- In a medium bowl, combine the diced pineapple, red bell pepper, red onion, jalapeño, and chopped cilantro.
- Add the fresh lime juice and a pinch of salt to taste.
- Gently toss to combine all the ingredients.
- Cover and refrigerate until ready to use.

3. **Preheat the Grill:**

- Preheat your grill to medium-high heat (about 400°F).
- Lightly oil the grill grates to prevent sticking.

4. **Grill the Tuna Steaks:**

- Remove the tuna steaks from the marinade, letting the excess marinade drip off.
- Place the tuna steaks on the preheated grill.
- Grill the tuna for about 2-3 minutes per side for medium-rare, or until the desired doneness is reached. Tuna steaks cook quickly, so keep an eye on them to avoid overcooking.

5. **Serve:**

- Transfer the grilled tuna steaks to a serving platter.
- Spoon the fresh pineapple salsa generously over the top of each tuna steak.

6. **Garnish and Enjoy:**

- Garnish with additional fresh cilantro leaves if desired.
- Serve the Grilled Tuna with Pineapple Salsa immediately, with extra lime wedges on the side for squeezing over the top.

Spicy Thai Shrimp Salad

Ingredients:

For the Shrimp:

- 1 pound large shrimp, peeled and deveined
- 2 tablespoons olive oil
- 1 tablespoon fresh lime juice (about 1 lime)
- 2 cloves garlic, minced
- 1 teaspoon chili powder
- Salt and freshly ground black pepper to taste

For the Spicy Thai Dressing:

- 1/4 cup fresh lime juice (about 2-3 limes)
- 2 tablespoons fish sauce
- 2 tablespoons soy sauce
- 2 tablespoons brown sugar
- 1 tablespoon rice vinegar
- 1 tablespoon sesame oil
- 1 tablespoon sriracha or Thai chili sauce (adjust to taste)
- 1 clove garlic, minced
- 1 tablespoon fresh ginger, grated

- 1/4 cup fresh cilantro, chopped

For the Salad:

- 6 cups mixed greens (such as romaine, arugula, spinach, and red leaf lettuce)
- 1 cup cherry tomatoes, halved
- 1/2 cucumber, sliced
- 1/2 red bell pepper, thinly sliced
- 1/4 red onion, thinly sliced
- 1/4 cup fresh cilantro leaves
- 1/4 cup fresh mint leaves
- 1/4 cup peanuts or cashews, chopped (optional)

1. **Marinate the Shrimp:**

- In a medium bowl, combine the olive oil, fresh lime juice, minced garlic, chili powder, salt, and pepper.
- Add the shrimp and toss to coat evenly.
- Cover and refrigerate for at least 15-30 minutes.

2. **Prepare the Spicy Thai Dressing:**

- In a small bowl, whisk together the fresh lime juice, fish sauce, soy sauce, brown sugar, rice vinegar, sesame oil, sriracha or Thai chili sauce, minced garlic, and grated ginger until well combined.
- Stir in the chopped fresh cilantro.
- Adjust the heat and seasoning to taste. Set aside.

3. **Preheat the Grill:**

- Preheat your grill to medium-high heat (about 375-400°F).
- Lightly oil the grill grates to prevent sticking.

4. **Grill the Shrimp:**

- Thread the marinated shrimp onto skewers for easier grilling, if desired.
- Place the shrimp on the preheated grill.

- Grill for about 2-3 minutes per side, or until the shrimp turn pink and opaque.
- Remove from the grill and set aside.

5. **Assemble the Salad:**

- In a large salad bowl, combine the mixed greens, cherry tomatoes, cucumber slices, red bell pepper slices, red onion, fresh cilantro leaves, and fresh mint leaves.
- Toss to mix the ingredients evenly.

6. **Add the Shrimp and Dressing:**

- Arrange the grilled shrimp on top of the salad.
- Drizzle the Spicy Thai Dressing over the salad and shrimp.
- Gently toss to coat the salad with the dressing.

7. **Serve:**

- Garnish the salad with chopped peanuts or cashews, if desired.
- Serve the Spicy Thai Shrimp Salad immediately.

Grilled Chicken and Pineapple Salad

Ingredients:

For the Chicken Marinade:

- 2 boneless, skinless chicken breasts
- 2 tablespoons olive oil
- 2 tablespoons fresh lime juice (about 1-2 limes)
- 2 cloves garlic, minced
- 1 teaspoon ground cumin
- 1 teaspoon smoked paprika
- Salt and freshly ground black pepper to taste

For the Pineapple:

- 1 fresh pineapple, peeled, cored, and cut into chunks

For the Citrus Vinaigrette:

- 1/4 cup fresh orange juice (about 1 orange)
- 2 tablespoons fresh lime juice (about 1-2 limes)
- 2 tablespoons olive oil
- 1 tablespoon honey or agave syrup

- 1 tablespoon Dijon mustard
- Salt and freshly ground black pepper to taste

For the Salad:

- 6 cups mixed greens (such as romaine, arugula, spinach, and red leaf lettuce)
- 1/2 red bell pepper, thinly sliced
- 1/2 cucumber, sliced
- 1/4 red onion, thinly sliced
- 1 avocado, sliced
- 1/4 cup fresh cilantro leaves
- 1/4 cup fresh mint leaves

1. **Marinate the Chicken:**

- In a small bowl, whisk together the olive oil, fresh lime juice, minced garlic, ground cumin, smoked paprika, salt, and pepper.
- Place the chicken breasts in a shallow dish or resealable plastic bag and pour the marinade over them, ensuring they are well coated.
- Cover and refrigerate for at least 30 minutes to 1 hour.

2. **Prepare the Citrus Vinaigrette:**

- In a small bowl, whisk together the fresh orange juice, fresh lime juice, olive oil, honey, Dijon mustard, salt, and pepper until well combined.
- Adjust seasoning to taste and set aside.

3. **Preheat the Grill:**

- Preheat your grill to medium-high heat (about 375-400°F).
- Lightly oil the grill grates to prevent sticking.

4. **Grill the Chicken and Pineapple:**

- Remove the chicken from the marinade and let the excess marinade drip off.
- Place the chicken breasts on the preheated grill.

- Grill the chicken for about 6-8 minutes per side, or until the internal temperature reaches 165°F and the chicken is no longer pink in the center.
- While the chicken is grilling, place the pineapple chunks on the grill.
- Grill the pineapple for about 2-3 minutes per side, or until caramelized and with nice grill marks.
- Remove the chicken and pineapple from the grill and let the chicken rest for a few minutes before slicing.

5. **Assemble the Salad:**

- In a large salad bowl, combine the mixed greens, red bell pepper slices, cucumber slices, red onion, avocado slices, fresh cilantro leaves, and fresh mint leaves.
- Toss to mix the ingredients evenly.

6. **Add the Grilled Chicken and Pineapple:**

- Slice the grilled chicken breasts into thin strips.
- Arrange the sliced chicken and grilled pineapple chunks on top of the salad.

7. **Dress the Salad:**

- Drizzle the citrus vinaigrette over the salad.
- Gently toss the salad to coat the ingredients with the dressing.

8. **Serve:**

- Serve the Grilled Chicken and Pineapple Salad immediately, with extra citrus vinaigrette on the side if desired.

Tropical Shrimp and Noodle Salad

Ingredients:

For the Salad:

- 8 ounces rice noodles
- 1 pound large shrimp, peeled and deveined
- 1 tablespoon olive oil
- 1 ripe mango, peeled and diced
- 1 cucumber, peeled, seeded, and julienned
- 1/2 red bell pepper, thinly sliced
- 1/4 cup fresh cilantro leaves, chopped
- 1/4 cup fresh mint leaves, chopped
- 2 green onions, thinly sliced
- 1 tablespoon sesame seeds (optional)

For the Spicy Lime Dressing:

- 1/4 cup fresh lime juice (about 2-3 limes)
- 2 tablespoons fish sauce
- 2 tablespoons soy sauce
- 2 tablespoons honey or agave syrup
- 1 tablespoon rice vinegar

- 1 tablespoon sesame oil
- 1 tablespoon sriracha or Thai chili sauce (adjust to taste)
- 1 clove garlic, minced
- 1 tablespoon fresh ginger, grated

1. **Cook the Rice Noodles:**

- Cook the rice noodles according to the package instructions. Drain and rinse under cold water to stop the cooking process. Set aside.

2. **Prepare the Shrimp:**

- In a medium bowl, toss the shrimp with olive oil, salt, and pepper.
- Heat a large skillet or grill pan over medium-high heat. Add the shrimp and cook for about 2-3 minutes per side, or until they turn pink and opaque.
- Remove from heat and set aside to cool slightly.

3. **Prepare the Spicy Lime Dressing:**

- In a small bowl, whisk together the fresh lime juice, fish sauce, soy sauce, honey, rice vinegar, sesame oil, sriracha or Thai chili sauce, minced garlic, and grated ginger until well combined.
- Adjust the heat and seasoning to taste.

4. **Assemble the Salad:**

- In a large salad bowl, combine the cooked rice noodles, cooked shrimp, diced mango, julienned cucumber, red bell pepper, chopped cilantro leaves, chopped mint leaves, and sliced green onions.
- Pour the spicy lime dressing over the salad ingredients.
- Gently toss to combine all the ingredients and coat them evenly with the dressing.

5. **Serve:**

- Transfer the Tropical Shrimp and Noodle Salad to a serving platter or individual bowls.
- Garnish with sesame seeds if desired.
- Serve immediately, or refrigerate for up to 30 minutes to let the flavors meld together.

Grilled Zucchini and Pesto Pasta

Ingredients:

For the Grilled Zucchini:

- 3 medium zucchinis, sliced lengthwise into 1/4-inch thick slices
- 2 tablespoons olive oil
- Salt and freshly ground black pepper to taste

For the Pesto Sauce:

- 2 cups fresh basil leaves, packed
- 1/2 cup grated Parmesan cheese
- 1/3 cup pine nuts (or walnuts)
- 2 cloves garlic
- 1/2 cup extra virgin olive oil
- Salt and freshly ground black pepper to taste

For the Pasta:

- 12 ounces pasta (such as penne, fusilli, or farfalle)
- 1/2 cup cherry tomatoes, halved (optional)
- 1/4 cup freshly grated Parmesan cheese, for serving

- Fresh basil leaves, for garnish

1. **Prepare the Pesto Sauce:**

- In a food processor, combine the fresh basil leaves, grated Parmesan cheese, pine nuts, and garlic.
- Pulse a few times until the ingredients are coarsely chopped.
- With the food processor running, slowly add the extra virgin olive oil in a steady stream until the pesto is well blended and smooth.
- Season with salt and freshly ground black pepper to taste.
- Set aside.

2. **Grill the Zucchini:**

- Preheat your grill to medium-high heat (about 375-400°F).
- Lightly brush the zucchini slices with olive oil on both sides.
- Season with salt and freshly ground black pepper.
- Place the zucchini slices on the preheated grill.
- Grill for about 2-3 minutes per side, or until tender and with nice grill marks.
- Remove from the grill and let cool slightly, then cut into bite-sized pieces.

3. **Cook the Pasta:**

- While the zucchini is grilling, cook the pasta according to the package instructions until al dente.
- Drain the pasta and reserve about 1/2 cup of the pasta cooking water.
- Rinse the pasta under cold water to stop the cooking process and set aside.

4. **Combine the Pasta and Pesto:**

- In a large bowl, toss the cooked pasta with the fresh pesto sauce.
- Add a bit of the reserved pasta cooking water, a tablespoon at a time, if needed, to thin the sauce and help it coat the pasta evenly.

5. **Assemble the Dish:**

- Add the grilled zucchini pieces and halved cherry tomatoes (if using) to the pasta.
- Gently toss to combine all the ingredients.

6. **Serve:**

- Transfer the Grilled Zucchini and Pesto Pasta to a serving platter or individual bowls.
- Garnish with freshly grated Parmesan cheese and fresh basil leaves.
- Serve immediately.

·

DRINK RECIPES
SUMMER

Classic Mojito

Ingredients:

- 10 fresh mint leaves, plus extra for garnish
- 1/2 lime, cut into 4 wedges
- 2 tablespoons white sugar, or to taste
- 1 cup ice cubes
- 1 1/2 ounces white rum
- 1/2 cup soda water (club soda or sparkling water)

1. **Muddle the Mint and Lime:**

- Place the mint leaves and 1 lime wedge into a sturdy glass.
- Use a muddler or the back of a spoon to crush the mint and lime to release the mint oils and lime juice.
- Add 2 more lime wedges and the sugar, and muddle again to release the lime juice.
- Do not strain the mixture.

2. **Add Ice and Rum:**

- Fill the glass almost to the top with ice cubes.
- Pour the white rum over the ice.

3. **Add Soda Water:**

- Add the soda water to the glass.
- Stir well to combine the ingredients and dissolve the sugar.

4. **Garnish and Serve:**

- Garnish with the remaining lime wedge and additional mint leaves.
- Serve immediately with a straw.

Strawberry Basil Lemonade

Ingredients:

For the Simple Syrup:

- 1 cup water
- 1 cup granulated sugar

For the Lemonade:

- 1 pound fresh strawberries, hulled and sliced
- 1/4 cup fresh basil leaves, plus extra for garnish
- 1 cup fresh lemon juice (about 6-8 lemons)
- 4 cups cold water
- 2 cups sparkling water
- Ice cubes
- Lemon slices, for garnish

1. **Prepare the Simple Syrup:**

- In a small saucepan, combine the water and granulated sugar.
- Bring to a simmer over medium heat, stirring until the sugar is completely dissolved.

- Remove from heat and let it cool to room temperature. This will make about 1 1/2 cups of simple syrup.

2. **Prepare the Strawberry Basil Mixture:**

- In a blender or food processor, combine the sliced strawberries and fresh basil leaves.
- Blend until smooth.
- Strain the mixture through a fine mesh sieve into a large pitcher to remove the seeds and basil bits. Use a spoon to press the mixture through the sieve to extract as much liquid as possible.

3. **Mix the Lemonade:**

- Add the fresh lemon juice to the pitcher with the strawberry basil mixture.
- Pour in the simple syrup (start with 1 cup and adjust to taste).
- Add the cold water and stir well to combine.

4. **Chill the Lemonade:**

- Refrigerate the lemonade for at least 1 hour to allow the flavors to meld and the lemonade to chill.

5. **Add Sparkling Water:**

- Just before serving, add the sparkling water to the pitcher and stir gently.

6. **Serve:**

- Fill glasses with ice cubes.
- Pour the Strawberry Basil Lemonade over the ice.
- Garnish each glass with lemon slices and fresh basil leaves.

Tropical Mango Margarita

Ingredients:

For the Mango Puree:

- 2 ripe mangoes, peeled, pitted, and diced
- 1/4 cup water
- 1 tablespoon lime juice

For the Margarita:

- 1 1/2 ounces tequila
- 1 ounce triple sec (orange liqueur)
- 2 ounces fresh lime juice (about 2 limes)
- 2 ounces mango puree (from above)
- 1/2 ounce simple syrup (adjust to taste)
- Ice cubes
- Salt or sugar for rimming the glass (optional)
- Lime wedges and mango slices, for garnish

1. **Prepare the Mango Puree:**

- In a blender, combine the diced mangoes, water, and lime juice.
- Blend until smooth.
- Strain the puree through a fine mesh sieve to remove any fibrous bits, if desired.
- Set aside. This will make about 1 cup of mango puree.

2. **Prepare the Glasses:**

- If desired, rim the glasses with salt or sugar.
- To do this, run a lime wedge around the rim of each glass, then dip the rim into a plate of salt or sugar to coat.
- Fill the glasses with ice cubes.

3. **Make the Margarita:**

- In a cocktail shaker, combine the tequila, triple sec, fresh lime juice, mango puree, and simple syrup.
- Fill the shaker with ice and shake vigorously for about 15 seconds until well chilled.

4. **Serve:**

- Strain the margarita into the prepared glasses over the ice.
- Garnish with lime wedges and mango slices.

5. **Adjust Sweetness:**

- Taste the margarita and adjust the sweetness by adding more simple syrup if desired.

Pineapple Coconut Rum Punch

Ingredients:

- 1 cup coconut rum
- 2 cups pineapple juice
- 1 cup orange juice
- 1/4 cup grenadine
- 1/4 cup fresh lime juice (about 2 limes)
- Ice cubes
- Pineapple slices and maraschino cherries, for garnish
- Orange slices, for garnish

1. **Prepare the Punch:**

- In a large pitcher, combine the coconut rum, pineapple juice, orange juice, and fresh lime juice.
- Stir well to mix all the ingredients together.

2. **Add Grenadine:**

- Slowly pour the grenadine into the mixture. It will sink to the bottom, creating a beautiful layered effect.
- Do not stir after adding the grenadine to maintain the layers.

3. **Chill the Punch:**

- Refrigerate the punch for at least 1 hour to allow the flavors to meld and the punch to chill.

4. **Serve:**

- Fill glasses with ice cubes.
- Slowly pour the punch into the glasses to maintain the layered effect.
- Garnish each glass with a pineapple slice, orange slice, and maraschino cherry.

Watermelon Mint Cooler

Ingredients:

- 6 cups fresh watermelon, cubed and seeds removed
- 1/4 cup fresh mint leaves, plus extra for garnish
- 1/2 cup fresh lime juice (about 4-5 limes)
- 1/2 cup vodka
- 2 tablespoons simple syrup (adjust to taste)
- Ice cubes
- Sparkling water (optional, for topping)
- Lime slices, for garnish

Instructions:

1. **Make the Watermelon Juice:**

- In a blender, combine the watermelon cubes and blend until smooth.
- Strain the watermelon puree through a fine mesh sieve into a large pitcher to remove any pulp. Use a spoon to press the mixture through the sieve to extract as much juice as possible. You should have about 4 cups of watermelon juice.

2. **Prepare the Mint and Lime:**

- In a small bowl, muddle the fresh mint leaves with the lime juice to release the mint's flavor.

3. **Mix the Cooler:**

- Add the muddled mint and lime juice mixture to the pitcher with the watermelon juice.
- Stir in the vodka and simple syrup until well combined.
- Taste and adjust the sweetness by adding more simple syrup if desired.

4. **Chill the Cooler:**

- Refrigerate the mixture for at least 1 hour to allow the flavors to meld and the cooler to chill.

5. **Serve:**

- Fill glasses with ice cubes.
- Pour the watermelon mint cooler over the ice.
- If desired, top with a splash of sparkling water for added fizz.
- Garnish each glass with extra mint leaves and lime slices.

Berry Sangria

Ingredients:

- 1 bottle (750 ml) red wine (such as Merlot, Rioja, or Cabernet Sauvignon)
- 1/2 cup brandy
- 1/4 cup orange liqueur (such as Triple Sec or Cointreau)
- 1/4 cup simple syrup (adjust to taste)
- 1 cup strawberries, hulled and sliced
- 1 cup blueberries
- 1 cup raspberries
- 1 orange, thinly sliced
- 1 lemon, thinly sliced
- 1 lime, thinly sliced
- 1 cup soda water (club soda or sparkling water)
- Ice cubes

1. **Prepare the Fruit:**

- Hull and slice the strawberries.
- Thinly slice the orange, lemon, and lime.
- Combine the strawberries, blueberries, raspberries, orange slices, lemon slices, and lime slices in a large pitcher.

2. **Mix the Sangria:**

- Pour the red wine, brandy, and orange liqueur over the mixed fruit in the pitcher.
- Add the simple syrup to the pitcher.
- Stir well to combine all the ingredients.

3. **Chill the Sangria:**

- Refrigerate the sangria for at least 2-4 hours, or preferably overnight, to allow the flavors to meld and the fruit to infuse the wine.

4. **Serve:**

- Before serving, add the soda water to the pitcher and stir gently.
- Fill glasses with ice cubes.
- Pour the berry sangria over the ice, making sure to include some of the mixed fruit in each glass.

5. **Garnish:**

- Garnish each glass with additional slices of orange, lemon, or lime, if desired.

Cucumber Gin and Tonic

Ingredients:

- 2 ounces gin
- 4 ounces tonic water
- 4-6 cucumber slices
- 1 lime wedge
- Ice cubes
- Cucumber slices and lime wheels, for garnish (optional)

1. **Prepare the Glass:**

- Fill a highball glass with ice cubes.
- Add 4-6 cucumber slices to the glass, layering them between the ice cubes.

2. **Add the Gin:**

- Pour 2 ounces of gin over the ice and cucumber slices.

3. **Add the Tonic Water:**

- Pour 4 ounces of tonic water into the glass, gently stirring to combine.

4. **Add the Lime:**

- Squeeze the juice from the lime wedge into the drink.
- Drop the lime wedge into the glass for extra flavor.

5. **Garnish and Serve:**

- Garnish with additional cucumber slices and lime wheels, if desired.
- Serve immediately.

Peach Bellini

Ingredients:

- 2 ripe peaches, peeled, pitted, and sliced
- 1 tablespoon fresh lemon juice
- 1 tablespoon simple syrup (adjust to taste)
- 1 bottle (750 ml) Prosecco, chilled

1. **Prepare the Peach Puree:**

- In a blender or food processor, combine the sliced peaches, fresh lemon juice, and simple syrup.
- Blend until smooth.
- Taste and adjust the sweetness by adding more simple syrup if desired.
- Strain the puree through a fine mesh sieve to remove any fibrous bits, if desired.

2. **Chill the Puree:**

- Transfer the peach puree to a container and refrigerate until cold, at least 1 hour.

3. **Assemble the Bellini:**

- For each serving, add about 2 tablespoons (1 ounce) of peach puree to a champagne flute.
- Slowly pour the chilled Prosecco over the puree, filling the glass.
- Gently stir to combine.

4. **Serve:**

- Garnish with a peach slice or a twist of lemon peel, if desired.
- Serve immediately.

Lemon Lavender Spritzer

Ingredients:

For the Lavender Syrup:

- 1 cup water
- 1 cup granulated sugar
- 2 tablespoons dried lavender flowers (culinary grade)

For the Spritzer:

- 1 1/2 ounces vodka
- 1 ounce fresh lemon juice (about 1 lemon)
- 1 ounce lavender syrup (from above)
- 4 ounces sparkling water
- Ice cubes
- Lemon slices, for garnish
- Fresh lavender sprigs, for garnish (optional)

1. **Prepare the Lavender Syrup:**

- In a small saucepan, combine the water and granulated sugar.

- Bring to a simmer over medium heat, stirring until the sugar is completely dissolved.
- Add the dried lavender flowers and remove from heat.
- Let the mixture steep for about 15 minutes.
- Strain the syrup through a fine mesh sieve to remove the lavender flowers.
- Allow the syrup to cool to room temperature.
- Store any leftover syrup in an airtight container in the refrigerator for up to 2 weeks.

2. **Prepare the Spritzer:**

- Fill a highball glass with ice cubes.
- Add the vodka, fresh lemon juice, and lavender syrup to the glass.
- Stir gently to combine.

3. **Add Sparkling Water:**

- Top off the glass with sparkling water, about 4 ounces.
- Stir gently to mix.

4. **Garnish and Serve:**

- Garnish with lemon slices and a fresh lavender sprig, if desired.
- Serve immediately.

Classic Margarita

Ingredients:

- 2 ounces tequila (preferably 100% agave)
- 1 ounce fresh lime juice (about 1 lime)
- 1 ounce triple sec (such as Cointreau or Grand Marnier)
- 1/2 ounce simple syrup (optional, for added sweetness)
- Ice cubes
- Lime wedge, for rimming the glass and garnish
- Coarse salt, for rimming the glass

1. **Prepare the Glass:**

- Run a lime wedge around the rim of a margarita or rocks glass.
- Dip the rim of the glass into a plate of coarse salt to coat the rim evenly.
- Fill the glass with ice cubes and set aside.

2. **Make the Margarita:**

- In a cocktail shaker, combine the tequila, fresh lime juice, triple sec, and simple syrup (if using).
- Fill the shaker with ice and shake vigorously for about 15 seconds until well chilled.

3. **Serve:**

- Strain the margarita into the prepared glass over the ice.
- Garnish with a lime wedge.

Ginger Lime Beer Cocktail

Ingredients:

- 12 ounces light beer (such as a lager or pilsner)
- 4 ounces ginger beer
- 1 ounce fresh lime juice (about 1 lime)
- Lime wedges, for garnish
- Ice cubes (optional)

1. **Prepare the Lime:**

- Cut a lime in half and juice one half to get about 1 ounce of fresh lime juice.
- Cut the other half into wedges for garnish.

2. **Mix the Cocktail:**

- In a large glass or beer mug, pour the fresh lime juice.
- Add the ginger beer and stir gently to combine.

3. **Add the Beer:**

- Slowly pour the light beer into the glass, allowing it to mix naturally with the ginger beer and lime juice.
- Stir gently if needed to combine.

4. **Serve:**

- If desired, add a few ice cubes to the glass to keep the drink extra cold.
- Garnish with a lime wedge on the rim of the glass.

Spicy Pineapple Jalapeño Margari

Ingredients:

- 2 ounces tequila (preferably 100% agave)
- 1 ounce triple sec (such as Cointreau or Grand Marnier)
- 2 ounces pineapple juice
- 1 ounce fresh lime juice (about 1 lime)
- 3-4 jalapeño slices (adjust to taste)
- 1/2 ounce simple syrup (optional, for added sweetness)
- Ice cubes
- Lime wedge, for rimming the glass and garnish
- Coarse salt, for rimming the glass
- Pineapple slice and jalapeño slice, for garnish (optional)

1. **Prepare the Glass:**

- Run a lime wedge around the rim of a margarita or rocks glass.
- Dip the rim of the glass into a plate of coarse salt to coat the rim evenly.
- Fill the glass with ice cubes and set aside.

2. **Muddle the Jalapeño:**

- In a cocktail shaker, add the jalapeño slices.
- Use a muddler or the back of a spoon to gently muddle the jalapeño slices to release their heat and flavor.

3. **Mix the Margarita:**

- Add the tequila, triple sec, pineapple juice, fresh lime juice, and simple syrup (if using) to the shaker with the muddled jalapeño.
- Fill the shaker with ice and shake vigorously for about 15 seconds until well chilled.

4. **Strain and Serve:**

- Strain the margarita into the prepared glass over the ice.
- Garnish with a lime wedge, a pineapple slice, and a jalapeño slice, if desired.

Raspberry Lime Rickey (Non-Alcoholic)

Ingredients:

- 1/2 cup fresh raspberries, plus extra for garnish
- 1 ounce fresh lime juice (about 1 lime)
- 1 ounce simple syrup (adjust to taste)
- 4 ounces club soda
- Ice cubes
- Lime wedges, for garnish

1. **Prepare the Lime:**

- Cut a lime in half and juice it to get about 1 ounce of fresh lime juice.
- Cut the other half into wedges for garnish.

2. **Muddle the Raspberries:**

- In a cocktail shaker or mixing glass, add the fresh raspberries and muddle them with the lime juice to release the juice and flavors from the berries.

3. **Add the Simple Syrup:**

- Add the simple syrup to the muddled raspberry and lime mixture.
- Stir to combine.

4. **Strain the Mixture:**

- Strain the raspberry-lime mixture into a glass filled with ice cubes to remove the seeds and pulp.

5. **Add Club Soda:**

- Slowly pour the club soda into the glass, stirring gently to combine.

6. **Garnish and Serve:**

- Garnish with a few fresh raspberries and a lime wedge.
- Serve immediately.

Minty Cucumber Lemonade (Non-Alcoholic)

Ingredients:

For the Simple Syrup:

- 1 cup water
- 1 cup granulated sugar

For the Lemonade:

- 1 large cucumber, thinly sliced
- 1/2 cup fresh mint leaves, plus extra for garnish
- 1 cup fresh lemon juice (about 4-6 lemons)
- 4 cups cold water
- 2 cups sparkling water
- Ice cubes
- Lemon slices, for garnish

1. **Prepare the Simple Syrup:**

- In a small saucepan, combine the water and granulated sugar.
- Bring to a simmer over medium heat, stirring until the sugar is completely dissolved.

- Remove from heat and let it cool to room temperature. This will make about 1 1/2 cups of simple syrup.

2. **Prepare the Lemonade:**

- In a large pitcher, combine the thinly sliced cucumber and fresh mint leaves.
- Using a muddler or the back of a wooden spoon, gently muddle the cucumber and mint to release their flavors.

3. **Mix the Lemonade:**

- Add the fresh lemon juice to the pitcher.
- Pour in the simple syrup (start with 1 cup and adjust to taste).
- Add the cold water and stir well to combine.

4. **Chill the Lemonade:**

- Refrigerate the lemonade for at least 1 hour to allow the flavors to meld and the lemonade to chill.

5. **Add Sparkling Water:**

- Just before serving, add the sparkling water to the pitcher and stir gently.

6. **Serve:**

- Fill glasses with ice cubes.
- Pour the Minty Cucumber Lemonade over the ice.
- Garnish each glass with extra mint leaves and lemon slices.

Tropical Fruit Smoothie (Non-Alcoholic)

Ingredients:

- 1 cup fresh pineapple chunks
- 1 cup fresh mango chunks
- 1 ripe banana
- 1 cup coconut milk (canned or carton)
- 1/2 cup orange juice (freshly squeezed if possible)
- 1 tablespoon honey or agave syrup (optional, for added sweetness)
- 1/2 cup ice cubes (optional, for a thicker smoothie)
- Pineapple slices or mango chunks, for garnish (optional)

1. **Prepare the Fruit:**

- Peel and chop the fresh pineapple and mango into chunks.
- Peel and slice the banana.

2. **Blend the Smoothie:**

- In a blender, combine the pineapple chunks, mango chunks, banana, coconut milk, and orange juice.
- If you prefer a sweeter smoothie, add the honey or agave syrup.
- Add the ice cubes if you want a thicker and colder smoothie.

3. **Blend Until Smooth:**

- Blend the ingredients on high speed until smooth and creamy.
- If the smoothie is too thick, add a bit more coconut milk or orange juice until you reach your desired consistency.

4. **Serve:**

- Pour the smoothie into glasses.
- Garnish with pineapple slices or mango chunks, if desired.
- Serve immediately.

FALL

Food: Savor the warmth with grilled sausages, roasted veggies, and savory pies. Infuse your dishes with the essence of fall - think apples and pumpkins.

Drinks: Warm your soul with spiced cocktails like apple cider sangria, cozy up with mulled wine, or savor the richness of a bourbon embrace. Rich, malty beers become your fall companions.

APPETIZERS & SIDE DISHES
FALL

Apple Cheddar Quesadillas

Ingredients:

- 2 large flour tortillas
- 1 cup shredded cheddar cheese
- 1 apple, thinly sliced
- 2 tablespoons butter

1. Heat a skillet over medium heat. Melt 1 tablespoon of butter.
2. Place one tortilla in the skillet. Sprinkle with half of the cheddar cheese, arrange apple slices on top, and add the remaining cheese.
3. Top with the second tortilla.
4. Cook until golden brown, then flip and cook the other side.
5. Remove from skillet and cut into wedges.

Pumpkin Hummus

Ingredients:

- 1 can chickpeas, drained and rinsed
- 1/2 cup pumpkin puree
- 2 tablespoons tahini
- 2 tablespoons olive oil
- 1 clove garlic
- 1 tablespoon lemon juice
- 1 teaspoon ground cumin
- 1/2 teaspoon smoked paprika
- Salt and pepper to taste

1. In a food processor, combine chickpeas, pumpkin puree, tahini, olive oil, garlic, lemon juice, cumin, smoked paprika, salt, and pepper. Blend until smooth.
2. Serve with pita bread or fresh vegetables.

Spiced Apple and Pecan Salad

Ingredients:

- 4 cups mixed greens
- 2 apples, thinly sliced
- 1/2 cup pecans, toasted
- 1/4 cup crumbled blue cheese
- 1/4 cup apple cider vinegar
- 2 tablespoons olive oil
- 1 tablespoon Dijon mustard
- 1 tablespoon honey
- Salt and pepper to taste

1. In a large bowl, combine mixed greens, apples, pecans, and blue cheese.
2. In a small bowl, whisk together apple cider vinegar, olive oil, Dijon mustard, honey, salt, and pepper. Drizzle over salad.

Roasted Pumpkin and Chickpea Salad

Ingredients:

- 2 cups pumpkin, peeled and cubed
- 1 can chickpeas, drained and rinsed
- 2 tablespoons olive oil
- 1 teaspoon ground cumin
- 1 teaspoon smoked paprika
- 4 cups arugula
- 1/4 cup tahini
- 2 tablespoons lemon juice
- 1 tablespoon honey
- Salt and pepper to taste

1. Preheat oven to 400°F.
2. Toss pumpkin and chickpeas with olive oil, cumin, smoked paprika, salt, and pepper. Roast for 25 minutes.
3. In a bowl, mix tahini, lemon juice, honey, salt, and pepper.
4. Toss arugula with roasted pumpkin, chickpeas, and tahini dressing.

Maple Pecan Sweet Potatoes

Ingredients:

- 4 sweet potatoes, peeled and cubed
- 2 tablespoons olive oil
- 1/4 cup maple syrup
- 1/2 cup chopped pecans
- 1 teaspoon ground cinnamon
- Salt and pepper to taste

1. Preheat oven to 400°F.
2. Toss sweet potatoes with olive oil, salt, and pepper. Roast for 25 minutes.
3. Drizzle with maple syrup, sprinkle with pecans and cinnamon. Roast for another 10 minutes.

Pumpkin Spice Energy Bites

Ingredients:

- 1 cup rolled oats
- 1/2 cup pumpkin puree
- 1/4 cup almond butter
- 1/4 cup honey
- 1/4 cup flaxseeds
- 1 teaspoon pumpkin pie spice
- 1/4 cup mini chocolate chips (optional)

1. In a bowl, combine rolled oats, pumpkin puree, almond butter, honey, flaxseeds, pumpkin pie spice, and mini chocolate chips (if using).
2. Mix well until combined.
3. Roll into bite-sized balls and refrigerate for at least 30 minutes before serving.

Caramelized Onion and Apple Tart

Ingredients:

- 1 sheet puff pastry
- 2 large onions, thinly sliced
- 2 apples, thinly sliced
- 2 tablespoons olive oil
- 1/2 cup crumbled goat cheese
- Fresh thyme for garnish

1. Preheat oven to 400°F.

2. In a skillet, caramelize onions in olive oil until golden brown.

3. Roll out puff pastry and top with caramelized onions, apple slices, and goat cheese.

4. Bake for 20-25 minutes. Garnish with fresh thyme.

Pear and Blue Cheese Flatbread

Ingredients:

- 1 pre-made flatbread
- 1 pear, thinly sliced
- 1/4 cup crumbled blue cheese
- 1/4 cup chopped walnuts
- 1 tablespoon honey
- Fresh arugula for garnish

1. Preheat oven to 400°F.
2. Arrange pear slices on the flatbread. Sprinkle with blue cheese and walnuts.
3. Bake for 10-12 minutes until flatbread is crispy and cheese is melted.
4. Drizzle with honey and garnish with fresh arugula.

Roasted Butternut Squash Soup

Ingredients:

- 1 butternut squash, peeled and cubed
- 1 large onion, chopped
- 3 garlic cloves, minced
- 4 cups vegetable broth
- 1 cup coconut milk
- 1 teaspoon ground nutmeg
- Salt and pepper to taste

1. Roast butternut squash in the oven at 400°F for 25 minutes.
2. In a pot, sauté onion and garlic until soft. Add roasted squash, vegetable broth, and bring to a boil.
3. Reduce heat and simmer for 20 minutes. Blend until smooth.
4. Stir in coconut milk, nutmeg, salt, and pepper. Serve hot.

Maple Glazed Brussels Sprouts

Ingredients:

- 1 pound Brussels sprouts, halved
- 2 tablespoons olive oil
- 1/4 cup maple syrup
- 2 tablespoons balsamic vinegar
- Salt and pepper to taste

1. Toss Brussels sprouts with olive oil, salt, and pepper. Roast at 400°F for 25 minutes.
2. Drizzle with maple syrup and balsamic vinegar. Roast for another 5 minutes.

Maple Glazed Carrots

Ingredients:

- 1 pound carrots, peeled and cut into sticks
- 2 tablespoons olive oil
- 1/4 cup maple syrup
- 2 tablespoons balsamic vinegar
- Salt and pepper to taste

1. Preheat oven to 400°F.
2. Toss carrots with olive oil, salt, and pepper. Roast for 20 minutes.
3. Drizzle with maple syrup and balsamic vinegar. Roast for another 10 minutes.

Roasted Root Vegetables with Honey Glaze

Ingredients:

- 1 large carrot, chopped
- 1 parsnip, chopped
- 1 sweet potato, chopped
- 1 beet, chopped
- 2 tablespoons olive oil
- 3 tablespoons honey
- Salt and pepper to taste

1. Toss vegetables with olive oil, salt, and pepper. Roast at 425°F for 30-35 minutes.
2. Drizzle with honey and roast for another 5 minutes.

Spaghetti Squash with Roasted Tomatoes and Pesto

Ingredients:

- 1 spaghetti squash
- 1 pint cherry tomatoes
- 2 tablespoons olive oil
- 1/4 cup pesto
- Salt and pepper to taste

1. Preheat oven to 400°F.
2. Cut spaghetti squash in half, remove seeds, and brush with olive oil. Season with salt and pepper. Roast cut side down for 40 minutes.
3. Toss cherry tomatoes with olive oil, salt, and pepper. Roast for 20 minutes.
4. Scrape out spaghetti squash strands with a fork. Toss with roasted tomatoes and pesto.

Cranberry Apple Slaw

Ingredients:

- 4 cups shredded cabbage
- 1 apple, julienned
- 1/2 cup dried cranberries
- 1/4 cup chopped pecans
- 1/4 cup Greek yogurt
- 2 tablespoons apple cider vinegar
- 1 tablespoon honey
- Salt and pepper to taste

1. In a large bowl, combine shredded cabbage, apple, cranberries, and pecans.
2. In a small bowl, whisk together Greek yogurt, apple cider vinegar, honey, salt, and pepper.
3. Pour dressing over slaw and toss to combine.

Roasted Beet and Goat Cheese Salad

Ingredients:

- 4 medium beets, roasted and sliced
- 4 cups mixed greens
- 1/4 cup crumbled goat cheese
- 1/4 cup chopped walnuts
- 2 tablespoons olive oil
- 1 tablespoon balsamic vinegar
- Salt and pepper to taste

1. Preheat oven to 400°F.
2. Toss beets with olive oil, salt, and pepper. Roast for 25-30 minutes until tender.
3. In a bowl, combine mixed greens, roasted beets, goat cheese, and walnuts.
4. Drizzle with olive oil and balsamic vinegar. Season with salt and pepper.

Apple Cinnamon Oatmeal Bake

Ingredients:

- 2 cups rolled oats
- 1 teaspoon baking powder
- 1 teaspoon ground cinnamon
- 1/2 teaspoon salt
- 2 cups milk (dairy or non-dairy)
- 1/2 cup applesauce
- 1/4 cup maple syrup
- 1 teaspoon vanilla extract
- 2 apples, peeled and chopped

1. Preheat oven to 350°F. Grease a baking dish.
2. In a large bowl, mix oats, baking powder, cinnamon, and salt.
3. In another bowl, whisk together milk, applesauce, maple syrup, and vanilla.
4. Pour wet ingredients into dry ingredients and mix well. Stir in chopped apples.
5. Pour mixture into the prepared baking dish. Bake for 35-40 minutes, until set and golden brown.

Pumpkin Spice Granola

Ingredients:

- 3 cups rolled oats
- 1 cup chopped nuts (pecans, walnuts, or almonds)
- 1/2 cup pumpkin seeds
- 1/4 cup honey or maple syrup
- 1/4 cup coconut oil, melted
- 1/2 cup pumpkin puree
- 1 teaspoon vanilla extract
- 2 teaspoons pumpkin pie spice
- 1/2 teaspoon salt

1. Preheat oven to 325°F.
2. In a large bowl, combine oats, nuts, and pumpkin seeds.
3. In a small bowl, mix honey, coconut oil, pumpkin puree, vanilla, pumpkin pie spice, and salt. Pour over oat mixture and stir to combine.
4. Spread mixture evenly on a baking sheet. Bake for 25-30 minutes, stirring halfway through, until golden brown.
5. Allow to cool completely before storing.

MAIN DISHES
FALL

Grilled Sausages with Apple Onion Relish

Ingredients:

- 6 sausages (bratwurst or Italian sausage)
- 2 large apples, peeled and thinly sliced
- 1 large onion, thinly sliced
- 2 tablespoons olive oil
- 2 tablespoons apple cider vinegar
- 1 tablespoon brown sugar
- Salt and pepper to taste

1. Grill the sausages until fully cooked.
2. In a skillet, heat olive oil over medium heat. Add onions and cook until translucent.
3. Add apple slices, apple cider vinegar, brown sugar, salt, and pepper. Cook until apples are tender.
4. Serve sausages with apple onion relish on top.

Apple Cider Chicken Thighs

Ingredients:

- 6 chicken thighs
- 1 cup apple cider
- 1/4 cup Dijon mustard
- 2 tablespoons olive oil
- 1 tablespoon fresh thyme leaves
- Salt and pepper to taste

1. Marinate chicken thighs in apple cider, Dijon mustard, olive oil, thyme, salt, and pepper for at least 1 hour.
2. Grill or bake at 375°F for 30-35 minutes until cooked through.

Pumpkin Ravioli with Sage Brown Butter

Ingredients:

- 1 package fresh pumpkin ravioli
- ¼ cup unsalted butter
- 8 fresh sage leaves
- Salt and pepper to taste
- Grated Parmesan cheese for serving

1. Cook ravioli according to package instructions.
2. In a skillet, melt butter over medium heat until it turns golden brown. Add sage leaves and cook until crispy.
3. Toss ravioli in the sage brown butter. Season with salt and pepper.
4. Serve with grated Parmesan cheese.

Grilled Pork Chops with Apple Cranberry Chutney

Ingredients:

- 4 pork chops
- 1 cup fresh cranberries
- 2 apples, peeled and diced
- 1/2 cup orange juice
- 1/4 cup brown sugar
- 1 teaspoon ground cinnamon
- Salt and pepper to taste

1. Grill pork chops until fully cooked.
2. In a saucepan, combine cranberries, apples, orange juice, brown sugar, and cinnamon. Cook until cranberries burst and apples are tender.
3. Serve pork chops with apple cranberry chutney.

Stuffed Acorn Squash

Ingredients:

- 2 acorn squashes, halved and seeds removed
- 1 cup cooked quinoa
- 1/2 cup dried cranberries
- 1/2 cup chopped walnuts
- 1/4 cup chopped parsley
- 2 tablespoons olive oil
- Salt and pepper to taste

1. Preheat oven to 375°F.
2. Drizzle olive oil over squash halves and season with salt and pepper. Roast for 40 minutes.
3. In a bowl, mix quinoa, cranberries, walnuts, parsley, salt, and pepper.
4. Stuff each squash half with quinoa mixture. Bake for another 10 minutes.

Pumpkin Sage Risotto

Ingredients:

- 1 cup Arborio rice
- 4 cups chicken or vegetable broth
- 1 cup pumpkin puree
- 1/2 cup grated Parmesan cheese
- 1/4 cup white wine
- 1 small onion, finely chopped
- 2 garlic cloves, minced
- 2 tablespoons butter
- 1 tablespoon fresh sage, chopped
- Salt and pepper to taste

1. In a pot, bring broth to a simmer.
2. In a large pan, melt butter and sauté onion and garlic until translucent. Add rice and cook until slightly toasted.
3. Add white wine and stir until absorbed. Add broth one ladle at a time, stirring frequently, until rice is creamy and cooked.
4. Stir in pumpkin puree, Parmesan cheese, sage, salt, and pepper. Serve hot.

Apple Cinnamon Pork Tenderloin

Ingredients:

- 1 pork tenderloin
- 2 apples, peeled and sliced
- 1/4 cup apple cider
- 2 tablespoons brown sugar
- 1 teaspoon ground cinnamon
- Salt and pepper to taste

1. Preheat oven to 375°F.
2. Season pork tenderloin with salt and pepper. Place in a baking dish.
3. In a bowl, mix apple slices, apple cider, brown sugar, and cinnamon. Pour over pork.
4. Bake for 25-30 minutes, until pork is cooked through.

Grilled Sausage and Pepper Skewers

Ingredients:

- 1 pound Italian sausage, cut into 1-inch pieces
- 2 red bell peppers, cut into 1-inch pieces
- 1 green bell pepper, cut into 1-inch pieces
- 1 yellow bell pepper, cut into 1-inch pieces
- 1 red onion, cut into 1-inch pieces
- 2 tablespoons olive oil
- Salt and pepper to taste

1. Preheat grill to medium-high heat.
2. Thread sausage, bell peppers, and onion onto skewers.
3. Brush with olive oil and season with salt and pepper.
4. Grill for 10-12 minutes, turning occasionally, until sausage is cooked and vegetables are tender.

Autumn Harvest Grain Bowl

Ingredients:

- 1 cup cooked farro or quinoa
- 1/2 cup roasted butternut squash
- 1/2 cup roasted Brussels sprouts
- 1/2 cup roasted beets
- 1/4 cup crumbled goat cheese
- 2 tablespoons chopped walnuts
- 2 tablespoons dried cranberries
- 2 tablespoons olive oil
- 1 tablespoon apple cider vinegar
- Salt and pepper to taste

1. In a bowl, combine cooked farro, roasted butternut squash, Brussels sprouts, beets, goat cheese, walnuts, and dried cranberries.
2. Drizzle with olive oil and apple cider vinegar. Season with salt and pepper.

Apple Pecan Stuffed Chicken Breasts

Ingredients:

- 4 boneless, skinless chicken breasts
- 1 apple, peeled and diced
- 1/4 cup chopped pecans
- 1/4 cup crumbled blue cheese
- 2 tablespoons olive oil
- Salt and pepper to taste

1. Preheat oven to 375°F.
2. Cut a pocket into each chicken breast.
3. In a bowl, combine apple, pecans, blue cheese, salt, and pepper.
4. Stuff each chicken breast with the apple mixture. Secure with toothpicks.
5. Heat olive oil in a skillet over medium-high heat. Sear chicken breasts on both sides until golden brown.
6. Transfer to the oven and bake for 20-25 minutes until cooked through.

Savory Pumpkin Pie

Ingredients:

- 1 pre-made pie crust
- 1 cup pumpkin puree
- 1/2 cup ricotta cheese
- 2 eggs
- 1 teaspoon dried thyme
- 1/2 teaspoon ground nutmeg
- Salt and pepper to taste

1. Preheat oven to 375°F.
2. In a bowl, mix pumpkin puree, ricotta cheese, eggs, thyme, nutmeg, salt, and pepper.
3. Pour mixture into pie crust. Bake for 35-40 minutes until set.

DRINK RECIPES
FALL

Apple Cider Sangria

Ingredients:

- 1 bottle white wine (such as Pinot Grigio)
- 2 cups apple cider
- 1/2 cup brandy
- 1/4 cup honey
- 1 apple, thinly sliced
- 1 pear, thinly sliced
- 1 orange, thinly sliced
- 1 cinnamon stick

1. In a pitcher, combine white wine, apple cider, brandy, and honey.
2. Add sliced apple, pear, orange, and cinnamon stick.
3. Stir well and refrigerate for at least 2 hours before serving.

Bourbon Apple Cider

Ingredients:

- 2 ounces bourbon
- 4 ounces apple cider
- 1/2 ounce fresh lemon juice
- 1/2 ounce simple syrup
- Ice cubes
- Apple slice and cinnamon stick, for garnish

1. In a cocktail shaker, combine bourbon, apple cider, lemon juice, and simple syrup. Shake well.
2. Fill a glass with ice cubes and pour the mixture over the ice.
3. Garnish with an apple slice and a cinnamon stick.

Spiced Pear Martini

Ingredients:

- 2 ounces vodka
- 1 ounce pear liqueur
- 1 ounce pear juice
- 1/2 ounce fresh lemon juice
- 1/2 ounce simple syrup
- Ice cubes
- Pear slice and cinnamon stick, for garnish

1. In a cocktail shaker, combine vodka, pear liqueur, pear juice, lemon juice, and simple syrup. Shake well with ice.
2. Strain into a chilled martini glass.
3. Garnish with a pear slice and a cinnamon stick.

Maple Old Fashioned

Ingredients:

- 2 ounces bourbon
- 1/2 ounce maple syrup
- 2 dashes Angostura bitters
- Ice cubes
- Orange twist and cherry, for garnish

1. In a mixing glass, combine bourbon, maple syrup, and Angostura bitters. Stir well with ice.
2. Strain into a rocks glass filled with ice.
3. Garnish with an orange twist and a cherry.

Caramel Apple Martini

Ingredients:

- 2 ounces vodka
- 1 ounce apple liqueur
- 1 ounce butterscotch schnapps
- 1 ounce apple cider
- Ice cubes
- Apple slice, for garnish

1. In a cocktail shaker, combine vodka, apple liqueur, butterscotch schnapps, and apple cider. Shake well with ice.
2. Strain into a chilled martini glass.
3. Garnish with an apple slice.

Pumpkin Spice Latte (Non-Alcoholic)

Ingredients:

- 2 cups milk (dairy or non-dairy)
- 2 tablespoons pumpkin puree
- 1 tablespoon sugar
- 1 tablespoon vanilla extract
- ½ teaspoon pumpkin pie spice
- ½ cup strong brewed coffee
- Whipped cream and ground cinnamon, for garnish

1. In a saucepan, combine milk, pumpkin puree, sugar, vanilla extract, and pumpkin pie spice. Heat until warm (do not boil).
2. Pour strong brewed coffee into a mug and add the pumpkin spice milk mixture.
3. Top with whipped cream and a sprinkle of ground cinnamon.

Cranberry Ginger Ale (Non-Alcoholic)

Ingredients:

- 1/2 cup cranberry juice
- 1/2 cup ginger ale
- 1/2 ounce fresh lime juice
- Ice cubes
- Fresh cranberries and lime wedge, for garnish

1. In a glass, combine cranberry juice, ginger ale, and fresh lime juice.
2. Add ice cubes and stir gently.
3. Garnish with fresh cranberries and a lime wedge.

Spiced Apple Punch (Non-Alcoholic)

Ingredients:

- 4 cups apple juice
- 1 cup orange juice
- 1/2 cup cranberry juice
- 1/4 cup fresh lemon juice
- 1 teaspoon ground cinnamon
- 1/2 teaspoon ground nutmeg
- Fresh apple slices and cinnamon sticks, for garnish

1. In a large pitcher, combine apple juice, orange juice, cranberry juice, fresh lemon juice, ground cinnamon, and ground nutmeg. Stir well.
2. Chill in the refrigerator for at least 1 hour.
3. Serve over ice and garnish with fresh apple slices and cinnamon sticks.

WINTER

Food: Comfort reigns supreme with barbecue pulled pork sandwiches, hearty soups, and indulgent cheese fondue. Celebrate winter's bounty with veggies like butternut squash and Brussels sprouts.

Drinks: Toast to robust red wines, steamy hot toddies, or creamy concoctions like Irish coffee. Dark beers and stouts boldly stand up to winter's hearty meals.

APPETIZERS & SIDE DISHES
WINTER

Butternut Squash Bruschetta

Ingredients:

- 1 baguette, sliced
- 2 cups butternut squash, peeled and cubed
- 2 tablespoons olive oil
- 1/4 cup ricotta cheese
- 1 tablespoon honey
- 1 teaspoon fresh thyme leaves
- Salt and pepper to taste

1. Preheat oven to 400°F.
2. Toss butternut squash with olive oil, salt, and pepper. Roast for 20-25 minutes until tender.
3. Toast baguette slices in the oven until golden brown.
4. Spread ricotta cheese on each slice, top with roasted squash, drizzle with honey, and sprinkle with thyme.

Spinach Artichoke Dip

Ingredients:

- 1 cup frozen spinach, thawed and drained
- 1 can artichoke hearts, drained and chopped
- 1 cup cream cheese
- 1/2 cup sour cream
- 1/2 cup grated Parmesan cheese
- 1/2 cup shredded mozzarella cheese
- 1 clove garlic, minced
- Salt and pepper to taste

1. Preheat oven to 375°F.
2. In a bowl, mix all ingredients until well combined.
3. Transfer to a baking dish and bake for 20-25 minutes until bubbly and golden brown.

Cheese Fondue

Ingredients:

- 1 clove garlic, halved
- 1 cup dry white wine
- 2 cups shredded Gruyère cheese
- 1 cup shredded Emmental cheese
- 1 tablespoon cornstarch
- 1 tablespoon lemon juice
- 1 tablespoon kirsch (cherry brandy)
- Salt, pepper, and nutmeg to taste

1. Rub the inside of a fondue pot with the garlic halves; discard garlic.
2. Heat wine over medium heat until simmering.
3. Toss cheese with cornstarch and add to pot, stirring until melted.
4. Stir in lemon juice, kirsch, salt, pepper, and nutmeg. Serve with bread cubes and veggies.

Roasted Brussels Sprouts with Balsamic Glaze

Ingredients:

- 1 pound Brussels sprouts, halved
- 2 tablespoons olive oil
- Salt and pepper to taste
- 1/4 cup balsamic vinegar
- 1 tablespoon honey

1. Preheat oven to 400°F.
2. Toss Brussels sprouts with olive oil, salt, and pepper. Roast for 20-25 minutes.
3. In a small saucepan, simmer balsamic vinegar and honey until reduced by half. Drizzle over roasted sprouts.

Sweet Potato Fries with Sriracha Aioli

Ingredients:

- 2 large sweet potatoes, cut into fries
- 2 tablespoons olive oil
- 1 teaspoon paprika
- Salt and pepper to taste
- 1/2 cup mayonnaise
- 1 tablespoon Sriracha sauce
- 1 teaspoon lemon juice

1. Preheat oven to 425°F.
2. Toss sweet potato fries with olive oil, paprika, salt, and pepper. Bake for 20-25 minutes until crispy.
3. Mix mayonnaise, Sriracha, and lemon juice for the aioli. Serve with fries.

Creamy Tomato Basil Soup

Ingredients:

- 1 tablespoon olive oil
- 1 onion, chopped
- 2 cloves garlic, minced
- 2 cans (28 oz each) crushed tomatoes
- 4 cups chicken or vegetable broth
- 1 cup heavy cream
- 1/4 cup fresh basil, chopped
- Salt and pepper to taste

1. In a pot, heat olive oil and sauté onion and garlic until soft.
2. Add tomatoes and broth, bring to a boil, then simmer for 20 minutes.
3. Stir in cream and basil. Blend until smooth. Season with salt and pepper.

Garlic Parmesan Knots

Ingredients:

- 1 can refrigerated biscuit dough
- 1/4 cup butter, melted
- 3 cloves garlic, minced
- 1/4 cup grated Parmesan cheese
- 1 tablespoon fresh parsley, chopped

1. Preheat oven to 375°F.
2. Cut each biscuit in half and roll into a rope. Tie into a knot.
3. Place on a baking sheet and bake for 10-12 minutes.
4. Mix melted butter, garlic, Parmesan, and parsley. Brush over warm knots.

Cranberry Pecan Brie Bites

Ingredients:

- 1 sheet puff pastry, thawed
- 1 wheel of Brie cheese, cut into small pieces
- 1/2 cup cranberry sauce
- 1/4 cup chopped pecans

1. Preheat oven to 375°F.
2. Cut puff pastry into small squares and place in a mini muffin tin.
3. Add a piece of Brie, a teaspoon of cranberry sauce, and a sprinkle of pecans to each.
4. Bake for 15-20 minutes until golden.

Roasted Garlic and Rosemary Focaccia

Ingredients:

- 3 cups all-purpose flour
- 1 teaspoon salt
- 1 packet active dry yeast
- 1 cup warm water
- 1/4 cup olive oil
- 2 cloves garlic, thinly sliced
- 1 tablespoon fresh rosemary, chopped
- Coarse sea salt

1. In a large bowl, combine flour, salt, and yeast.
2. Add warm water and olive oil, mix until a dough forms. Knead for 5 minutes.
3. Place dough in an oiled bowl, cover, and let rise for 1 hour.
4. Preheat oven to 400°F. Press dough into a baking pan, dimple with fingers, and top with garlic, rosemary, and sea salt.
5. Bake for 20-25 minutes until golden brown.

Winter Harvest Salad

Ingredients:

- 4 cups mixed greens
- 1 apple, thinly sliced
- 1/2 cup roasted butternut squash cubes
- 1/4 cup dried cranberries
- 1/4 cup crumbled goat cheese
- 1/4 cup candied pecans
- 1/4 cup balsamic vinaigrette

1. In a large bowl, combine mixed greens, apple, butternut squash, cranberries, goat cheese, and pecans.
2. Drizzle with balsamic vinaigrette and toss to combine.

MAIN DISHES
WINTER

Barbecue Pulled Pork Sandwiches

Ingredients:

- 3 pounds pork shoulder
- 1 cup barbecue sauce
- 1/2 cup apple cider vinegar
- 1/4 cup brown sugar
- 1 tablespoon smoked paprika
- 1 tablespoon garlic powder
- 1 tablespoon onion powder
- Salt and pepper to taste
- Burger buns

1. Rub pork shoulder with smoked paprika, garlic powder, onion powder, salt, and pepper.
2. Place in a slow cooker with barbecue sauce, apple cider vinegar, and brown sugar. Cook on low for 8 hours.
3. Shred pork and serve on burger buns with additional barbecue sauce.

Beef and Barley Stew

Ingredients:

- 1 pound beef stew meat
- 1 tablespoon olive oil
- 1 onion, chopped
- 3 carrots, chopped
- 3 celery stalks, chopped
- 3 cloves garlic, minced
- 6 cups beef broth
- 1 cup barley
- 1 teaspoon dried thyme
- 1 teaspoon dried rosemary
- Salt and pepper to taste

1. In a large pot, heat olive oil and brown beef stew meat.
2. Add onion, carrots, celery, and garlic, sauté until soft.
3. Add beef broth, barley, thyme, rosemary, salt, and pepper. Bring to a boil, then simmer for 1 hour.

Grilled Chicken with Lemon Herb Butter

Ingredients:

- 4 chicken breasts
- 2 tablespoons olive oil
- Salt and pepper to taste
- 1/4 cup butter, softened
- 2 tablespoons fresh lemon juice
- 1 tablespoon fresh parsley, chopped
- 1 teaspoon fresh thyme, chopped

1. Preheat grill to medium-high heat.
2. Brush chicken breasts with olive oil, salt, and pepper. Grill for 6-8 minutes per side until cooked through.
3. Mix butter, lemon juice, parsley, and thyme. Serve chicken topped with lemon herb butter.

Baked Ziti with Sausage

Ingredients:

- 1 pound Italian sausage, casings removed
- 1 onion, chopped
- 3 cloves garlic, minced
- 1 jar marinara sauce
- 1 pound ziti pasta
- 1 cup ricotta cheese
- 2 cups shredded mozzarella cheese
- 1/4 cup grated Parmesan cheese
- Fresh basil for garnish

1. Preheat oven to 375°F.
2. Cook ziti according to package instructions. Drain and set aside.
3. In a large skillet, cook sausage, onion, and garlic until sausage is browned.
4. Add marinara sauce and simmer for 10 minutes.
5. In a large bowl, combine cooked ziti, sausage mixture, ricotta, and half of the mozzarella.
6. Transfer to a baking dish, top with remaining mozzarella and Parmesan. Bake for 20-25 minutes until bubbly.
7. Garnish with fresh basil.

Slow Cooker Chicken and Dumplings

Ingredients:

- 4 boneless, skinless chicken breasts
- 1 onion, chopped
- 3 carrots, chopped
- 3 celery stalks, chopped
- 3 cloves garlic, minced
- 4 cups chicken broth
- 1 cup frozen peas
- 1 cup heavy cream
- 2 cups biscuit mix
- 2/3 cup milk
- Salt and pepper to taste

1. Place chicken, onion, carrots, celery, garlic, and chicken broth in a slow cooker. Cook on low for 6 hours.
2. Shred chicken and return to slow cooker. Add peas and heavy cream.
3. Mix biscuit mix and milk, drop by spoonfuls into the slow cooker. Cook on high for 1 hour until dumplings are cooked through.

Shepherd's Pie

Ingredients:

- 1 pound ground lamb or beef
- 1 onion, chopped
- 3 carrots, chopped
- 3 cloves garlic, minced
- 1 cup frozen peas
- 1 cup beef broth
- 2 tablespoons tomato paste
- 2 tablespoons Worcestershire sauce
- 4 cups mashed potatoes
- 1/4 cup shredded cheddar cheese
- Salt and pepper to taste

1. Preheat oven to 400°F.
2. In a skillet, cook ground lamb or beef, onion, carrots, and garlic until meat is browned.
3. Add peas, beef broth, tomato paste, Worcestershire sauce, salt, and pepper. Simmer for 10 minutes.
4. Transfer to a baking dish, top with mashed potatoes and cheddar cheese. Bake for 20 minutes until golden.

Grilled Lamb Chops with Mint Pesto

Ingredients:

- 8 lamb chops
- 2 tablespoons olive oil
- Salt and pepper to taste
- 1 cup fresh mint leaves
- 1/4 cup pine nuts
- 1/4 cup grated Parmesan cheese
- 1/4 cup olive oil
- 2 cloves garlic

1. Preheat grill to medium-high heat.
2. Brush lamb chops with olive oil, salt, and pepper. Grill for 3-4 minutes per side until desired doneness.
3. In a food processor, combine mint, pine nuts, Parmesan, olive oil, and garlic. Blend until smooth. Serve lamb chops with mint pesto.

Turkey and Wild Rice Casserole

Ingredients:

- 2 cups cooked turkey, shredded
- 1 cup wild rice, cooked
- 1 onion, chopped
- 2 celery stalks, chopped
- 2 cloves garlic, minced
- 1 can cream of mushroom soup
- 1/2 cup sour cream
- 1/2 cup shredded cheddar cheese
- 1/4 cup chopped parsley
- Salt and pepper to taste

1. Preheat oven to 350°F.
2. In a skillet, sauté onion, celery, and garlic until soft.
3. In a large bowl, combine turkey, wild rice, sautéed vegetables, cream of mushroom soup, sour cream, salt, and pepper.
4. Transfer to a baking dish, top with cheddar cheese and parsley. Bake for 25-30 minutes until bubbly.

Beef Stroganoff

Ingredients:

- 1 pound beef sirloin, thinly sliced
- 1 onion, chopped
- 3 cloves garlic, minced
- 1 cup mushrooms, sliced
- 1 cup beef broth
- 1/2 cup sour cream
- 2 tablespoons flour
- 2 tablespoons butter
- 1 tablespoon Dijon mustard
- 1 tablespoon Worcestershire sauce
- Salt and pepper to taste
- Egg noodles, cooked

1. In a skillet, melt butter and sauté onion, garlic, and mushrooms until soft.
2. Add beef sirloin and cook until browned.
3. Sprinkle flour over beef and stir well. Add beef broth, Dijon mustard, Worcestershire sauce, salt, and pepper. Simmer for 10 minutes.
4. Stir in sour cream and cook until heated through. Serve over egg noodles.

DRINK RECIPES
WINTER

Hot Toddy (Winter Edition)

Ingredients:

- 2 ounces whiskey
- 1 tablespoon honey
- 1 tablespoon fresh lemon juice
- 1 cup hot water
- Lemon slice and cinnamon stick, for garnish

1. In a mug, combine whiskey, honey, and fresh lemon juice.
2. Top with hot water and stir well.
3. Garnish with a lemon slice and a cinnamon stick.

Irish Coffee

Ingredients:

- 1 cup hot coffee
- 1 tablespoon brown sugar
- 1 1/2 ounces Irish whiskey
- Whipped cream, for garnish

1. In a mug, combine hot coffee, brown sugar, and Irish whiskey. Stir well.
2. Top with whipped cream and serve.

Bourbon Hot Chocolate

Ingredients:

- 2 cups milk
- 1/4 cup cocoa powder
- 1/4 cup sugar
- 1/4 cup dark chocolate, chopped
- 2 ounces bourbon
- Whipped cream and chocolate shavings, for garnish

1. In a saucepan, heat milk, cocoa powder, and sugar over medium heat until warm.
2. Add dark chocolate and stir until melted.
3. Remove from heat and stir in bourbon. Serve with whipped cream and chocolate shavings.

Spiked Eggnog

Ingredients:

- 4 cups eggnog
- 1 cup rum or bourbon
- 1/2 teaspoon ground nutmeg
- Whipped cream and ground cinnamon, for garnish

1. In a pitcher, combine eggnog, rum or bourbon, and ground nutmeg. Stir well.
2. Serve with whipped cream and a sprinkle of ground cinnamon.

Apple Cider Bourbon Cocktail

Ingredients:

- 2 ounces bourbon
- 4 ounces apple cider
- 1/2 ounce fresh lemon juice
- 1/2 ounce simple syrup
- Ice cubes
- Apple slice and cinnamon stick, for garnish

1. In a cocktail shaker, combine bourbon, apple cider, lemon juice, and simple syrup. Shake well.
2. Fill a glass with ice cubes and pour the mixture over the ice.
3. Garnish with an apple slice and a cinnamon stick.

Dark and Stormy

Ingredients:

- 2 ounces dark rum
- 3 ounces ginger beer
- 1/2 ounce fresh lime juice
- Lime wedge, for garnish

1. Fill a glass with ice cubes.
2. Add dark rum and lime juice. Top with ginger beer.
3. Stir gently and garnish with a lime wedge.

Hot Chocolate with Marshmallows (Non-Alcoholic)

Ingredients:

- 2 cups milk
- 1/4 cup cocoa powder
- 1/4 cup sugar
- 1/4 cup dark chocolate, chopped
- Marshmallows, for garnish

1. In a saucepan, heat milk, cocoa powder, and sugar over medium heat until warm.
2. Add dark chocolate and stir until melted.
3. Serve with marshmallows.

Spiced Apple Cider (Non-Alcoholic)

Ingredients:

- 4 cups apple cider
- 2 cinnamon sticks
- 4 cloves
- 2 star anise
- Orange slices, for garnish

1. In a saucepan, combine apple cider, cinnamon sticks, cloves, and star anise.
2. Heat over medium heat until warm. Let the flavors infuse for 15 minutes.
3. Serve with orange slices.

Gingerbread Latte (Non-Alcoholic)

Ingredients:

- 1 cup milk
- 1/2 cup strong brewed coffee
- 1 tablespoon molasses
- 1 tablespoon sugar
- 1/2 teaspoon ground ginger
- 1/2 teaspoon ground cinnamon
- Whipped cream and ground nutmeg, for garnish

1. In a saucepan, heat milk, molasses, sugar, ground ginger, and ground cinnamon over medium heat until warm.
2. Pour strong brewed coffee into a mug and add the milk mixture.
3. Top with whipped cream and a sprinkle of ground nutmeg.

Peppermint Hot Chocolate (Non-Alcoholic)

Ingredients:

- 2 cups milk
- 1/4 cup cocoa powder
- 1/4 cup sugar
- 1/4 cup dark chocolate, chopped
- 1/2 teaspoon peppermint extract
- Whipped cream and crushed candy canes, for garnish

1. In a saucepan, heat milk, cocoa powder, and sugar over medium heat until warm.
2. Add dark chocolate and stir until melted.
3. Stir in peppermint extract. Serve with whipped cream and crushed candy canes.

Cranberry Spritzer (Non-Alcoholic)

Ingredients:

- 1 cup cranberry juice
- 1 cup sparkling water
- 1/2 ounce fresh lime juice
- Ice cubes
- Fresh cranberries and lime wedge, for garnish

1. In a glass, combine cranberry juice, sparkling water, and fresh lime juice.
2. Add ice cubes and stir gently.
3. Garnish with fresh cranberries and a lime wedge.

SPRING

Food: Welcome the renewal of spring with grilled chicken salads, colorful vegetable skewers, and light pastas dressed in pesto or zesty lemon sauces. Spring vegetables like asparagus and peas add a fresh crunch.

Drinks: Sip on light and floral cocktails such as lavender lemonade spritzer, cucumber gin and tonic, or a fruity white sangria. Crisp beers and sparkling wines are the toast of springtime.

Disclaimer: *Tailor your menu to delight the palates of your guests. And remember, hydration is key – always offer a range of non-alcoholic options and plenty of water, especially when the sun is out.*

Now, let's dive into the heart of Poolside Cooking™ - the recipes that make every season taste like summer.

APPETIZERS & SIDE DISHES
SPRING

Grilled Asparagus with Lemon Aioli

Ingredients:

- 1 pound asparagus, trimmed
- 2 tablespoons olive oil
- Salt and pepper to taste
- 1/2 cup mayonnaise
- 1 tablespoon lemon juice
- 1 teaspoon lemon zest
- 1 garlic clove, minced

1. Preheat grill to medium-high heat.
2. Toss asparagus with olive oil, salt, and pepper. Grill for 4-5 minutes until tender.
3. Mix mayonnaise, lemon juice, lemon zest, and garlic to make aioli. Serve with grilled asparagus.

Spring Pea and Mint Crostini

Ingredients:

- 1 baguette, sliced
- 1 cup fresh peas
- 1/4 cup fresh mint leaves
- 1/4 cup ricotta cheese
- 2 tablespoons olive oil
- Salt and pepper to taste

1. Preheat oven to 375°F. Toast baguette slices until golden brown.
2. Blanch peas in boiling water for 2 minutes, then plunge into ice water.
3. In a food processor, blend peas, mint, ricotta, olive oil, salt, and pepper until smooth. Spread on crostini.

Lemon Herb Ricotta Stuffed Mushrooms

Ingredients:

- 24 large mushrooms, stems removed
- 1 cup ricotta cheese
- 2 tablespoons fresh parsley, chopped
- 1 tablespoon fresh dill, chopped
- 1 tablespoon lemon zest
- 1 garlic clove, minced
- Salt and pepper to taste

1. Preheat oven to 375°F.
2. Mix ricotta, parsley, dill, lemon zest, garlic, salt, and pepper.
3. Stuff mushroom caps with ricotta mixture. Bake for 20-25 minutes until mushrooms are tender.

Spring Vegetable Quinoa Salad

Ingredients:

- 1 cup quinoa
- 2 cups water
- 1 cup diced cucumber
- 1 cup cherry tomatoes, halved
- 1/2 cup radishes, thinly sliced
- 1/4 cup red onion, finely chopped
- 1/4 cup fresh parsley, chopped
- 1/4 cup olive oil
- 2 tablespoons lemon juice
- Salt and pepper to taste

1. Rinse quinoa and cook in water according to package instructions. Let cool.
2. In a large bowl, combine quinoa, cucumber, tomatoes, radishes, red onion, and parsley.
3. In a small bowl, whisk olive oil, lemon juice, salt, and pepper. Pour over salad and toss.

Grilled Zucchini Roll-Ups with Goat Cheese

Ingredients:

- 2 large zucchinis, sliced lengthwise into thin strips
- 2 tablespoons olive oil
- Salt and pepper to taste
- 1/2 cup goat cheese, softened
- 2 tablespoons fresh basil, chopped
- 1 tablespoon lemon zest

1. Preheat grill to medium-high heat.
2. Brush zucchini slices with olive oil, salt, and pepper. Grill for 2-3 minutes per side.
3. Mix goat cheese, basil, and lemon zest. Spread on zucchini slices and roll up.

Strawberry Spinach Salad with Balsamic Glaze

Ingredients:

- 4 cups baby spinach
- 1 cup strawberries, sliced
- 1/4 cup red onion, thinly sliced
- 1/4 cup feta cheese, crumbled
- 1/4 cup walnuts, toasted
- 1/4 cup balsamic glaze

1. In a large bowl, combine spinach, strawberries, red onion, feta cheese, and walnuts.
2. Drizzle with balsamic glaze and toss to combine.

Lemon Dill Hummus

Ingredients:

- 1 can chickpeas, drained and rinsed
- 1/4 cup tahini
- 2 tablespoons lemon juice
- 1 tablespoon lemon zest
- 2 tablespoons fresh dill, chopped
- 2 garlic cloves, minced
- 1/4 cup olive oil
- Salt and pepper to taste

1. In a food processor, combine chickpeas, tahini, lemon juice, lemon zest, dill, garlic, and olive oil. Blend until smooth.
2. Season with salt and pepper. Serve with pita chips or fresh vegetables.

Carrot and Ginger Soup

Ingredients:

- 1 tablespoon olive oil
- 1 onion, chopped
- 3 cloves garlic, minced
- 1 tablespoon fresh ginger, grated
- 6 carrots, peeled and sliced
- 4 cups vegetable broth
- 1 cup coconut milk
- Salt and pepper to taste

1. In a pot, heat olive oil and sauté onion, garlic, and ginger until soft.
2. Add carrots and vegetable broth. Bring to a boil, then simmer for 20 minutes until carrots are tender.
3. Blend until smooth. Stir in coconut milk and season with salt and pepper.

MAIN DISHES
SPRING

Grilled Chicken Salad with Citrus Vinaigrette

Ingredients:

- 4 chicken breasts
- 2 tablespoons olive oil
- Salt and pepper to taste
- 4 cups mixed greens
- 1 orange, segmented
- 1/4 cup red onion, thinly sliced
- 1/4 cup feta cheese, crumbled
- 1/4 cup pecans, toasted
- 1/4 cup olive oil
- 2 tablespoons fresh orange juice
- 1 tablespoon Dijon mustard
- 1 tablespoon honey

1. Preheat grill to medium-high heat.
2. Brush chicken breasts with olive oil, salt, and pepper. Grill for 6-8 minutes per side until cooked through. Slice.
3. In a large bowl, combine mixed greens, orange segments, red onion, feta cheese, and pecans.
4. In a small bowl, whisk olive oil, orange juice, Dijon mustard, and honey. Pour over salad and toss. Top with grilled chicken.

Lemon Pesto Pasta with Spring Vegetables

Ingredients:

- 1 pound pasta (penne or fusilli)
- 2 cups asparagus, cut into 1-inch pieces
- 1 cup peas
- 1/2 cup cherry tomatoes, halved
- 1/2 cup basil pesto
- 1/4 cup lemon juice
- 1 tablespoon lemon zest
- 1/4 cup grated Parmesan cheese
- Salt and pepper to taste

1. Cook pasta according to package instructions. Drain and set aside.
2. Blanch asparagus and peas in boiling water for 2 minutes, then plunge into ice water.
3. In a large bowl, combine pasta, asparagus, peas, cherry tomatoes, pesto, lemon juice, and lemon zest. Toss well.
4. Sprinkle with Parmesan cheese and season with salt and pepper.

Grilled Salmon with Dill Yogurt Sauce

Ingredients:

- 4 salmon fillets
- 2 tablespoons olive oil
- Salt and pepper to taste
- 1 cup Greek yogurt
- 2 tablespoons fresh dill, chopped
- 1 tablespoon lemon juice
- 1 tablespoon lemon zest

1. Preheat grill to medium-high heat.
2. Brush salmon fillets with olive oil, salt, and pepper. Grill for 4-5 minutes per side until cooked through.
3. In a small bowl, mix Greek yogurt, dill, lemon juice, and lemon zest. Serve with grilled salmon.

Spring Vegetable Stir-Fry

Ingredients:

- 2 tablespoons olive oil
- 1 red bell pepper, sliced
- 1 yellow bell pepper, sliced
- 1 cup snap peas
- 1 cup asparagus, cut into 1-inch pieces
- 1 cup mushrooms, sliced
- 2 garlic cloves, minced
- 1 tablespoon soy sauce
- 1 tablespoon hoisin sauce
- 1 tablespoon fresh ginger, grated

1. In a large skillet or wok, heat olive oil over medium-high heat.
2. Add bell peppers, snap peas, asparagus, mushrooms, and garlic. Stir-fry for 5-7 minutes until vegetables are tender-crisp.
3. Stir in soy sauce, hoisin sauce, and ginger. Cook for another 2 minutes. Serve hot.

Grilled Shrimp Tacos with Mango Salsa

Ingredients:

- 1 pound shrimp, peeled and deveined
- 2 tablespoons olive oil
- 1 tablespoon chili powder
- 1 teaspoon garlic powder
- 1 teaspoon cumin
- Salt and pepper to taste
- 8 small tortillas
- 1 mango, diced
- 1/2 red onion, finely chopped
- 1/4 cup fresh cilantro, chopped
- 1 tablespoon lime juice
- Salt and pepper to taste

1. Preheat grill to medium-high heat.
2. Toss shrimp with olive oil, chili powder, garlic powder, cumin, salt, and pepper. Grill for 2-3 minutes per side.
3. In a bowl, combine mango, red onion, cilantro, lime juice, salt, and pepper to make salsa.
4. Serve shrimp in tortillas topped with mango salsa.

Lemon Herb Grilled Chicken

Ingredients:

- 4 chicken breasts
- 1/4 cup olive oil
- 2 tablespoons lemon juice
- 1 tablespoon lemon zest
- 1 tablespoon fresh rosemary, chopped
- 1 tablespoon fresh thyme, chopped
- 1 garlic clove, minced
- Salt and pepper to taste

1. Preheat grill to medium-high heat.
2. In a bowl, mix olive oil, lemon juice, lemon zest, rosemary, thyme, garlic, salt, and pepper.
3. Marinate chicken breasts in the mixture for at least 30 minutes.
4. Grill for 6-8 minutes per side until cooked through.

Grilled Vegetable Skewers with Balsamic Glaze

Ingredients:

- 1 zucchini, sliced
- 1 yellow squash, sliced
- 1 red onion, cut into wedges
- 1 red bell pepper, cut into chunks
- 1 yellow bell pepper, cut into chunks
- 2 tablespoons olive oil
- Salt and pepper to taste
- 1/4 cup balsamic vinegar
- 1 tablespoon honey

1. Preheat grill to medium-high heat.
2. Thread zucchini, yellow squash, red onion, and bell peppers onto skewers.
3. Brush with olive oil, salt, and pepper. Grill for 8-10 minutes, turning occasionally.
4. In a small saucepan, simmer balsamic vinegar and honey until reduced by half. Drizzle over grilled vegetables.

Spinach and Ricotta Stuffed Chicken Breasts

Ingredients:

- 4 chicken breasts
- 1 cup fresh spinach, chopped
- 1/2 cup ricotta cheese
- 1/4 cup grated Parmesan cheese
- 1 garlic clove, minced
- 1 tablespoon fresh basil, chopped
- Salt and pepper to taste

1. Preheat oven to 375°F.
2. In a bowl, mix spinach, ricotta, Parmesan, garlic, basil, salt, and pepper.
3. Cut a pocket into each chicken breast and stuff with the ricotta mixture. Secure with toothpicks.
4. Place in a baking dish and bake for 25-30 minutes until cooked through.

Lemon Garlic Shrimp Pasta

Ingredients:

- 1 pound pasta (linguine or spaghetti)
- 1 pound shrimp, peeled and deveined
- 2 tablespoons olive oil
- 4 garlic cloves, minced
- 1/4 cup lemon juice
- 1 tablespoon lemon zest
- 1/4 cup fresh parsley, chopped
- 1/4 cup grated Parmesan cheese
- Salt and pepper to taste

1. Cook pasta according to package instructions. Drain and set aside.
2. In a large skillet, heat olive oil over medium heat. Add garlic and cook until fragrant.
3. Add shrimp and cook for 2-3 minutes per side until pink.
4. Stir in lemon juice, lemon zest, salt, and pepper. Toss with cooked pasta.
5. Sprinkle with parsley and Parmesan cheese.

Spring Pea Risotto

Ingredients:

- 1 cup Arborio rice
- 4 cups chicken or vegetable broth
- 1 cup fresh peas
- 1/2 cup dry white wine
- 1 onion, finely chopped
- 2 garlic cloves, minced
- 2 tablespoons olive oil
- 1/4 cup grated Parmesan cheese
- 1/4 cup fresh mint, chopped
- Salt and pepper to taste

1. In a pot, heat broth and keep warm.
2. In a large pan, heat olive oil and sauté onion and garlic until soft. Add rice and cook until slightly toasted.
3. Add white wine and stir until absorbed. Add broth one ladle at a time, stirring frequently, until rice is creamy and cooked.
4. Stir in peas, Parmesan cheese, mint, salt, and pepper. Serve hot.

DRINK RECIPES
SPRING

Cucumber Mint Gin Fizz

Ingredients:

- 2 ounces gin
- 1/2 ounce fresh lime juice
- 1/2 ounce simple syrup
- 4 cucumber slices
- 6 fresh mint leaves
- Club soda
- Ice cubes
- Cucumber slice and mint sprig for garnish

1. Muddle cucumber slices and mint leaves in a shaker.
2. Add gin, lime juice, simple syrup, and ice. Shake well.
3. Strain into a glass filled with ice and top with club soda.
4. Garnish with a cucumber slice and mint sprig.

Strawberry Basil Martini

Ingredients:

- 2 ounces vodka
- 1 ounce fresh lime juice
- 1 ounce simple syrup
- 4 strawberries, hulled
- 4 basil leaves
- Ice cubes
- Strawberry and basil leaf for garnish

1. Muddle strawberries and basil leaves in a shaker.
2. Add vodka, lime juice, simple syrup, and ice. Shake well.
3. Strain into a chilled martini glass.
4. Garnish with a strawberry and basil leaf.

White Peach Sangria

Ingredients:

- 1 bottle white wine (such as Sauvignon Blanc)
- 1/2 cup peach schnapps
- 1/4 cup brandy
- 1/4 cup simple syrup
- 2 peaches, sliced
- 1 orange, sliced
- 1 cup strawberries, hulled and sliced
- 1/4 cup fresh mint leaves
- Club soda
- Ice cubes

Instructions:

1. In a pitcher, combine white wine, peach schnapps, brandy, simple syrup, peaches, orange, strawberries, and mint leaves.
2. Chill for at least 2 hours.
3. Serve over ice and top with club soda.

Rose Spritzer

Ingredients:

- 1 bottle rosé wine
- 1 cup club soda
- 1/4 cup fresh lemon juice
- 1/4 cup elderflower liqueur
- Ice cubes
- Lemon slices and fresh berries for garnish

1. In a pitcher, combine rosé wine, club soda, lemon juice, and elderflower liqueur. Stir well.
2. Serve over ice and garnish with lemon slices and fresh berries.

Grapefruit Rosemary Gin Cocktail

Ingredients:

- 2 ounces gin
- 1 ounce fresh grapefruit juice
- 1/2 ounce rosemary simple syrup
- Club soda
- Ice cubes
- Grapefruit slice and rosemary sprig for garnish

1. In a shaker, combine gin, grapefruit juice, rosemary simple syrup, and ice. Shake well.
2. Strain into a glass filled with ice and top with club soda.
3. Garnish with a grapefruit slice and rosemary sprig.

Kiwi Lime Mojito

Ingredients:

- 2 ounces white rum
- 1 ounce fresh lime juice
- 1/2 ounce simple syrup
- 1 kiwi, peeled and sliced
- 6 fresh mint leaves
- Club soda
- Ice cubes
- Kiwi slice and mint sprig for garnish

1. Muddle kiwi slices and mint leaves in a shaker.
2. Add rum, lime juice, simple syrup, and ice. Shake well.
3. Strain into a glass filled with ice and top with club soda.
4. Garnish with a kiwi slice and mint sprig.

Lavender Lemonade Spritzer (Non-alcoholic)

Ingredients:

- 1 cup water
- 1 cup sugar
- 2 tablespoons dried lavender flowers
- 1 cup fresh lemon juice
- 4 cups sparkling water
- Ice cubes
- Lemon slices and lavender sprigs for garnish

1. In a saucepan, combine water, sugar, and lavender. Bring to a simmer until sugar dissolves. Let cool and strain.
2. In a pitcher, combine lavender syrup, lemon juice, and sparkling water. Stir well.
3. Serve over ice and garnish with lemon slices and lavender sprigs.

Honeydew Mint Lemonade (Non-alcoholic)

Ingredients:

- 1 cup honeydew melon, cubed.
- 1/4 cup fresh lemon juice
- 1/4 cup simple syrup
- 6 fresh mint leaves
- 2 cups water
- Ice cubes
- Honeydew slice and mint sprig for garnish

1. In a blender, puree honeydew melon until smooth. Strain through a fine mesh sieve.
2. In a pitcher, combine honeydew juice, lemon juice, simple syrup, mint leaves, and water. Stir well.
3. Serve over ice and garnish with a honeydew slice and mint sprig.

Cucumber Mint Cooler (Non-alcoholic)

Ingredients:

- 1 cucumber, sliced
- 1/4 cup fresh lime juice
- 1/4 cup simple syrup
- 6 fresh mint leaves
- 2 cups sparkling water
- Ice cubes
- Cucumber slice and mint sprig for garnish

1. In a blender, puree cucumber until smooth. Strain through a fine mesh sieve.
2. In a pitcher, combine cucumber juice, lime juice, simple syrup, mint leaves, and sparkling water. Stir well.
3. Serve over ice and garnish with a cucumber slice and mint sprig.

Raspberry Mint Iced Tea (Non-alcoholic)

Ingredients:

- 1 cup raspberries
- 1/4 cup fresh lime juice
- 1/4 cup simple syrup
- 6 fresh mint leaves
- 4 cups brewed black tea, chilled
- Ice cubes
- Raspberries and mint sprig for garnish

1. In a blender, puree raspberries until smooth. Strain through a fine mesh sieve.
2. In a pitcher, combine raspberry juice, lime juice, simple syrup, mint leaves, and black tea. Stir well.
3. Serve over ice and garnish with raspberries and a mint sprig.

Watermelon Lime Agua Fresca (Non-alcoholic)

Ingredients:

- 2 cups watermelon, cubed
- 1/4 cup fresh lime juice
- 1/4 cup simple syrup
- 2 cups water
- Ice cubes
- Watermelon slice and lime wheel for garnish

1. In a blender, puree watermelon until smooth. Strain through a fine mesh sieve.
2. In a pitcher, combine watermelon juice, lime juice, simple syrup, and water. Stir well.
3. Serve over ice and garnish with a watermelon slice and lime wheel.

LIFESTYLE TIPS for the POOLSIDE CONNOISSEUR

When we say Poolside Cooking™ is a lifestyle, we mean it. Beyond mere recipes, it's about cultivating an atmosphere of relaxation and connection. Let's dive into the lifestyle tips that ensure you live the Poolside Cooking™ life to its fullest.

1. The Art of Relaxation

Cooking poolside is an invitation to unwind. Let the rhythm of chopping and sizzling sync with the tranquility of water nearby. Music also adds to the ambiance. It's about enjoying the culinary journey as much as the destination.

2. Communal Connections

Use poolside cooking as an opportunity to connect with others. Invite friends, family, and neighbors to share in the experience, fostering a sense of community. Use episodes from our TV show to receive inspiration on how to add the Poolside Cooking™ lifestyle to spice up your life, community, and home.

3. Seasonal Sensibility

A seasonal approach to cuisine isn't just trendy; it's tasty. Source ingredients at their peak to ensure your dishes burst with natural, full-bodied flavors. Trust us, your guests will thank you.

4. Creative Cocktails

Let your imagination flow like a fine libation. Create signature drinks that complement your culinary creations. Whether it's a zesty sangria or a mocktail, pair your dishes with drinks that enhance the poolside palate. Our TV show can be your muse for mixology.

5. Sustainable and Local Choices

Conscious cooking starts with ingredient selection. Support the local ecosystem by choosing farmers' markets and consider a garden of your own for the freshest herbs and veggies.

6. Versatile Menus

Diversity in diet welcomes all to the table. Design menus that cater to different dietary preferences and restrictions, ensuring that everyone can indulge in the poolside culinary experience. If you follow our show over the years, you know we are all about tasty cuisine from vegan to carnivores and everyone in between, to guarantee a universally enjoyable dining experience.

7. Effortless Elegance

A poolside meal should be as pleasing to the eye as to the palate. Set the scene with stylish tableware, comfortable seating, and ambient lighting for a chic but relaxed atmosphere.

8. Mindful Hosting

Attentive hosting means anticipating needs. Be mindful of your guests' needs and preferences. Have options for both alcoholic and non-alcoholic beverages, and consider dietary restrictions when planning the menu.

9. Safety First

Prioritize safety, especially when combining water activities with cooking. Ensure a designated cooking area away from the pool's edge, and be cautious with open flames or hot surfaces. Remember, you want to ensure that every memory is a happy one.

10. Savor the Moment

Poolside Cooking™ is not just about the food; it's about creating lasting memories. If you watch our show, you know the fun times we have and the diverse guests and conversations. Emulate the joy seen on our show: keep the phones away, put away distractions, enjoy good company, and savor the moments spent by the pool.

11. Elevating Everyday Moments

With a dash of poolside panache, even a simple Tuesday dinner can feel like a celebration. Transform ordinary moments into extraordinary experiences. Whether it's a weekday dinner or a weekend gathering, let every meal be a chance to elevate the ordinary into the sublime.

12. Balance and Well-being

Wellness is a recipe best shared. Balance indulgence with nourishment, and let the poolside be your retreat for both feasting and feeling good.

Remember, the essence of Poolside Cooking™ is not just about the meals; it's about cultivating a lifestyle that celebrates good food, good company, and the joy of shared moments by the water.

FROM POOLSIDE to PLATE:
Tips for Hosting the Ultimate Poolside Gathering

Creating an unforgettable poolside gathering is an art form that combines ambiance, flavor, and the joy of togetherness. Here's how you can set the scene for a splendid affair:

1. **Plan with Purpose:** Begin with a vision for your gathering. Consider the occasion, the number of guests, and the type of experience you want to create. A thought-out plan ensures a seamless event.

2. **Invitations and Expectations:** Set the tone with personalized invitations that hint at the theme and dress code. Encourage guests to dress comfortably but stylishly to blend in with the poolside elegance.

3. **Music and Mood:** Curate a playlist that complements the theme of your gathering. Whether it's tropical tunes for a luau or jazz for a more sophisticated soirée, music is a crucial element in creating the right mood.

4. **Pool Prep:** Make sure the pool is clean and well-maintained. Add floaties or inflatables for a playful touch, and consider ambient lighting for when the sun sets.

5. **Culinary Delights:** Offer a variety of dishes that cater to different tastes and dietary requirements. The key is to balance simplicity with sophistication, allowing guests to savor the flavors without the need for complex utensils or plates.

6. **Refreshment Station:** Set up a drinks station with a selection of beverages. Include creative mocktails, fresh juices, and infused waters alongside spirited options.

7. **Activity Agenda:** While the pool is the main attraction, not all guests may want to swim. Arrange for other activities like poolside games, dancing, a photo booth, or even a mini outdoor movie area.

8. **Parting Gifts:** Send your guests home with a token of appreciation that reflects the theme of the party, such as a personalized towel, a mini sunscreen, or a recipe card from the menu.

DECORATING YOUR POOLSIDE SPACE
Themes and Inspirations

Creating an inviting and themed poolside space is essential for setting the tone for your gathering. A well-decorated area not only delights the eyes but also enhances the overall experience of your guests. Here are some themes and inspirations to transform your poolside into a picturesque setting:

Tropical Oasis

Imagine stepping into a scene straight from a sun-kissed beach in the Caribbean. To achieve this look:

Color Palette: Utilize bright colors like turquoise, sunny yellow, and coral.

Decor: Scatter palm fronds and tropical flowers. Consider inflatable palm trees or flamingos for a touch of whimsy.

Lighting: String lights with tropical motifs like pineapples or coconuts can add a warm glow as the sun sets.

Mediterranean Retreat

Evoke the tranquil and luxurious feel of a Mediterranean villa with these ideas:

Color Palette: Choose sea blues, white, and sandy tones to reflect the coastal theme.

Decor: Use terracotta pots with olive trees or lavender. Incorporate mosaic tiles on tabletops.

Lighting: Lanterns with candles can cast a soft, inviting light that mimics the setting sun on a Mediterranean coastline.

Garden Party Elegance

For a more sophisticated vibe, a garden party theme is perfect:

Color Palette: Soft pastels, floral patterns, and plenty of greens.

Decor: Fresh flowers, decorative bird cages, and elegant tablecloths can set a refined yet relaxed scene.

Lighting: Opt for fairy lights woven through greenery and centerpieces with candles for a subtle, enchanting effect.

Nautical Chic

Capture the spirit of the seaside with a nautical theme:

Color Palette: Navy, stripes, and crisp whites with red accents for contrast.

Decor: Use ropes, anchors, and starfish as decor elements. Striped cushions and throws can add comfort and style.

Lighting: Blue and white lanterns or lamps shaped like lighthouses keep the theme cohesive and functional.

Rustic Country BBQ

For a casual and cozy atmosphere, go rustic:

Color Palette: Earthy tones, deep reds, and denim blues.
Decor: Wooden tables, checkered tablecloths, and wildflowers in mason jars create a homey feel.
Lighting: Edison bulbs hanging from wooden structures or wrapped around trees provide a warm, rustic charm.

Boho Chic

Embrace a relaxed and artistic vibe with a Boho Chic theme:

Color Palette: Mix and match vibrant colors with earth tones for a bohemian look.

Decor: Use eclectic textiles, patterned rugs, and plush floor cushions for seating.

Lighting: Moroccan lanterns or colored glass votives can scatter beautiful patterns and soft light around the pool.

Vintage Glamour

Step back in time to an era of old-school Hollywood glamour:

Color Palette: Black, white, with metallic gold or silver accents.
Decor: Use feather boas, pearl strands, and mirrored trays to evoke a sense of 1920s luxury.
Lighting: Chandeliers or candelabras with flickering candles can add a touch of vintage elegance.

Zen Minimalist

For a serene and modern setting, minimalism is key:

Color Palette: Neutral colors with accents of deep green or stone grey.
Decor: Simple, clean lines with water features like a tabletop fountain and smooth stones.
Lighting: Understated LED candles or bamboo torches can maintain the tranquil atmosphere.

When decorating your poolside space, always consider the comfort of your guests. Ensure there's ample seating, shaded areas, and that your decor creates a cohesive and inviting environment. Let your chosen theme guide the mood and transport your guests to whatever splendid setting you choose to emulate.

MAKING YOUR POOLSIDE PARTY INCLUSIVE and WELCOMING

The hallmark of a great host is the ability to make every guest feel welcome and included. Here are some strategies to ensure everyone has a memorable time:

- **Understanding Inclusivity**

Inclusivity means ensuring everyone feels valued and welcome, regardless of their background, beliefs, or abilities. An inclusive poolside party is one where all guests can participate and enjoy the event to the fullest.

- **Diversity in Invitations**

When creating your guest list, consider a diverse mix of individuals. Invite people from different walks of life - varying cultures, ages, and social backgrounds. This diversity enriches the gathering and encourages a blend of perspectives and experiences.

- **Accessibility Matters**

Ensure that your poolside area is accessible to everyone, including guests with mobility challenges. Have clear pathways, ramps instead of steps if possible, and seating arrangements that can accommodate wheelchairs or walkers.

- **Menu for All**

Offer a variety of food options catering to different dietary needs and preferences such as vegetarian, vegan, gluten-free, and halal. Clearly label dishes and consider potential food allergies.

- **Non-Alcoholic Options**

While poolside gatherings often feature cocktails and drinks, provide an array of non-alcoholic beverages. This consideration ensures that those who do not drink alcohol, whether for personal, health, or religious reasons, can still enjoy a special beverage.

- **Cultural Sensitivity**

Be mindful of cultural sensitivities and holidays. Try not to schedule your party on significant cultural or religious dates unless the theme of the party is to celebrate that specific occasion with respect.

- **Activities for Everyone**

Plan activities that are not just water-centric. Not everyone may want to swim. Include games, music, and other forms of entertainment that allow all guests to engage and interact.

- **Personal Touches**

Tailor aspects of the party to your guests. This could mean customizing the menu to accommodate allergies or including cultural touches that resonate with the diversity of your invitees.

- **Comfort is Crucial:**

Ensure there are plenty of shaded areas, seating options, and accessibility for all guests. Comfortable and inclusive spaces allow everyone to relax and enjoy the event.

- **Quiet Spaces**

Some guests might appreciate a space away from the crowd to relax or have a quiet conversation. Set up a lounge area with comfortable seating away from the main party zone.

- **Child-Friendly Zones**

If children are part of your guest list, ensure there's a safe and fun space for them to play. Consider hiring a lifeguard if children will be swimming, to put parents at ease.

- **Clear Communication**

Communicate any specific details about the party beforehand. This includes mentioning accessibility, outlining the event's schedule, and describing the food and drink options available. This allows guests to prepare and know what to expect.

- **Warm Welcomes**

As the host, make an effort to greet each guest personally. Introduce them to others to encourage mingling and conversation. This can be through ice-breaker games, shared dining tables, or group activities. Your warmth and hospitality set the tone for the entire event.

- **Feedback Loop**

After the event, seek feedback from your guests on their experience. This will help you understand what worked well and what could be improved to make future gatherings even more inclusive and enjoyable.

Remember, the goal of inclusivity is to create a space where every guest leaves feeling like they were a valued part of the celebration. Each element, from planning to farewell, contributes to a poolside party that's not just a gathering, but a cherished memory. Keep these tips in mind to turn your next poolside event from a simple splash into a sophisticated and inclusive soiree that celebrates the best of food, decor, and company.

AFTERWORD

Remember, Poolside Cooking™ is a lifestyle. Join the movement!
PoolsideCookingShow.com
Coming Soon:

Poolside Cooking Cafe
3877 Holland Rd, Suite 510, Virginia Beach, VA 23452